JANE AUSTEN
&
THE AUSTEN FAMILY

The Poetry of Jane Austen and the Austen Family

Edited by David Selwyn

University of Iowa Press, Iowa City
In association with
the Jane Austen Society

CONTENTS

PREFACE

This volume of verse by the Austen family contains all the known poems of Jane Austen herself and a selection of those written by, among others, her sister Cassandra, four of her brothers, her uncle James Leigh Perrot, her nieces Anna and Fanny and her nephew James Edward. It is clear that her mother must have had a considerable influence on Jane Austen's verse-writing; Mrs Austen was a skilful and witty practitioner whose efforts are unfailingly delightful, and all her extant poems have been included. As is explained in the Introduction, verses were often written as part of a game, with various members of the family making their own contribution to a round of charades or bouts-rimés; although generally the items in the book are grouped separately by author, I have included a section with three sets of verses arranged in this way.

The texts are taken from autograph manuscripts, or, where no autograph exists, from the earliest known copy to survive; they have been transcribed exactly as they stand in the original, with no alterations to spelling, punctuation or layout, except for quotation marks, which are given as single throughout. The Austens frequently copied out verses for circulation and where more than one autograph exists, significant variants from the one printed are given in the Textual Notes. In the case of Jane Austen's poems all variants are given; since no MS of any of her major novels has survived (the two cancelled chapters of *Persuasion* apart), anything in her hand merits the closest scrutiny. The notes also give details of first publication, though some of the verses have long been out of print; where no such date is given, the verse is published here for the first time.

A general description of the kinds of verse the family wrote, as well as some biographical details, will be found in the Introduction. Each poem has a brief headnote, and at the end of the volume a fuller account will by found in the Explanatory Notes, where reference is made to other works, in particular to relevant passages in Jane Austen's novels and letters.

I very much hope that this book, which offers for the first time a collection of the verses that three generations of the Austen family composed largely for their own amusement, will at once give pleasure to the general reader and provide for the scholar an insight into a largely neglected aspect of Jane Austen's writing.

DAVID SELWYN, 1996

INTRODUCTION

When James Stanier Clarke, the Prince Regent's domestic chaplain, suggested to Jane Austen that she might consider writing a 'historical romance, illustrative of the history of the august House of Cobourg', she replied that she 'could no more write a romance than an epic poem'. Even allowing for the fact that her letter was dated 1 April, the remark is not just a disclaimer to any ambitions as a chronicler of European royalty but a clear denial of poetic ability. Yet, as in many households of the late eighteenth century, writing verse was something of a pastime with the Austens and the composition of ingenious riddles and charades provided a source of lively entertainment.

Jane Austen's mother, in particular, was a keen participant in these activities. At the age of six she had been described by her uncle Theophilus Leigh, the Master of Balliol, as 'already the poet of the family', and after her marriage to the Revd George Austen she retained her delight in verse as a means of deriving amusement from the commonplaces of daily existence, whether it was a complaint from her husband's young pupils about being kept awake by the scraping of the rectory weathercock, or the list of guests at a ball sent to an absent daughter, or the recipe for a pudding turned into verse and copied into the household cookery book. In the lines she wrote while recovering from a serious illness she could even find comedy in a brush with death. Mrs Austen's distinctive tone of voice – good-humoured, intelligent and abounding in practical common sense – is clearly audible in everything she wrote.

Mrs Austen's wealthy brother, James Leigh Perrot (he added the 'Perrot' to his name on inheriting a family estate), shared her facility, though he confined himself largely to writing riddles and charades, as was the case with her two youngest sons, the 'sailor brothers', Francis William and Charles John. Cassandra, too, seems to have written very little; the three verses by her that are known will be found in the present volume. Edward Austen (later Knight), the third son, was not, so far as is known, of a literary turn. Having been adopted heir by Thomas Knight of Godmersham Park in Kent, where Jane and Cassandra were frequent visitors, his time was largely devoted to running his estates, which, as well as Godmersham, comprised property in Hampshire at Steventon and Chawton (the widowed Mrs Austen, with her daughters and their friend Martha Lloyd, moved into a house in the latter in 1809). Two of his children – George Knight and Jane's favourite niece, Fanny – did however acquire the family habit of writing verse.

To the Austens' eldest son James and his brother Henry literature was of considerable importance. During their period together at St John's College, Oxford, they published jointly a weekly magazine, *The Loiterer*, which ran for sixty numbers between January 1789 and March 1790. Henry, who had three careers, as an adjutant in the army, a banker and, following the failure of his business, a clergyman, subsequently wrote little except sermons and the 'Biographical Notice' of Jane Austen at the beginning of the posthumously published *Northanger Abbey* and *Persuasion* (though a poem about Godmersham is included here). James, however, became a prolific, if unpublished, poet, whose works reflect both a gift for light verse and an aspiration to serious nature poetry in the manner of Gray's 'Elegy' or Thomson's *Seasons*. The selection in the present volume represents only a small proportion of more than forty poems, some quite lengthy, copied into two albums after his death by his son, James Edward Austen-Leigh.

It was James Austen who wrote the verse prologues and epilogues for the plays that were acted at Steventon rectory in Jane Austen's childhood. Between 1782 and 1789 there were regular theatrical performances by the family and their friends, either in the dining-room or in the barn on the other side of the road; among the many plays produced were Fielding's *Tom Thumb* and Sheridan's *The Rivals*. (A generation later there were similar theatricals at Godmersham, for which Jane Austen herself made a burlesque adaptation of Richardson's *Sir Charles Grandison*.) Ordained in 1787, James eventually succeeded his father as rector of Steventon. His elder daughter, Anna, another niece close to Jane Austen, began a novel which was much discussed with her aunt; and in later life, as widow of the Revd Ben Lefroy, she published several improving children's books. Caroline, who with James Edward was a child of James Austen's second marriage, to Mary Lloyd, wrote down memories of her visits to Chawton that have provided invaluable material for Austen biographers.

In his *Memoir of Jane Austen* (1870) James Edward Austen-Leigh tells us that amongst his aunt's favourite writers 'Johnson in prose, Crabbe in verse, and Cowper in both, stood high', and it is quite clear from references in the novels and letters that she knew Crabbe, Thomson, Gray, Pope, Milton and Shakespeare, as well as her contemporaries Byron and Scott. She often makes judicious use of these poets to reveal something of a character's social or intellectual development: Elinor Dashwood in *Sense and Sensibility* jokingly tells Marianne that Mr Willoughby admires Pope 'no more than is proper'; in *Northanger Abbey* the young Catherine Morland has read 'all such works as heroines must read to supply their memories with those quotations which are so serviceable and so soothing in the vicissitudes of their eventful lives'; and Sir Edward Denham, in *Sanditon*, makes such a hopeless confusion of Scott, Campbell and Blair, in his attempts to impress the eminently sensible Charlotte Heywood with the depth of his feeling for literature, that she thinks him 'downright silly'. Even the clever Emma Woodhouse, interpreting Mr Elton's charade for Harriet, misinterprets it in one important respect – she thinks it is directed at Harriet, when really it is intended for herself.

Jane Austen's own verse has much in common with the lighter pieces published in the *Gentleman's Magazine* and the various miscellanies that appeared throughout the century, of which the most important was Dodsley's (we know that she had a copy of this from a letter in which she tells Cassandra that she has sold it for ten shillings). She probably also possessed another popular anthology of the day, *Elegant Extracts*, since it contains a witty little squib on the Universities of which there exists a copy in her hand:

> No wonder that Oxford and Cambridge profound
> In Learning and Science so greatly abound
> Since some *carry* thither a little each day
> And we meet with so few that *bring any away*.

Her verses, like those of Mrs Austen, were often suggested by domestic matters. They could serve, for example, as a gift-tag accompanying some pocket-handkerchiefs or a little work-bag; they could record a headache or a visit to the doctor. They could offer the opportunity for congratulations on a marriage or comfort in a bereavement, without the necessity of dwelling unduly on the serious side of either. How clearly Jane Austen made the distinction between being a poet and being a novelist is seen in her comments on Scott, who, she said, had 'no business to write novels, especially good ones. It is not fair. He has fame and profit enough as a poet and should not be taking the bread out of other people's mouths.' So it is only in an ironic sense that she saw herself as a poet. In the verses on Mr Best, who refused to escort Martha Lloyd to Harrogate, the mock immodesty of the phrase 'tuneful poet' draws attention to her real identity, which is that of a moralist, neatly pinning down the inconsistency of Mr Best's refusal and citing unanswerable reasons for his not persisting in it. Similarly, the poem written when Anna had been experiencing some adolescent difficulties hints at a critique of her niece's character that comes close to her art as a novelist; and the verse letter congratulating Francis William on the birth of a son is a testament to that fraternal love which is described in *Mansfield Park* as being 'sometimes almost every thing... at others worse than nothing'.

Some element of the public world can occasionally be glimpsed in the verse. In a letter to Godmersham she includes a short poem congratulating Edward on a delay in the Weald of Kent Canal Bill, to which he was opposed – though the point, naturally, lies in her brother's concern rather than in the parliamentary bill itself. Even a piece of genuine satire, aimed at the reprimand delivered by court martial on the naval commander Home Riggs Popham, may have had a personal interest: Popham lived at

Sonning in Berkshire, where a brother-in-law of Mrs Austen had been rector and he would also have been known to Francis Austen through the Navy.

In the one attempt to express her feelings seriously in verse, 'To the Memory of Mrs Lefroy', her diction is plain, prosaic almost, and couched in the faintly cold language of religious memorial tablets. Anne Lefroy, wife of the Rector of Ashe, near Steventon, had been almost a second mother to her; she was killed in a fall from a horse on Jane Austen's birthday, 16 December 1804, and it was the unhappy coincidence of the date that, four years later, prompted the poem. The language of mourning can hardly have come naturally, and the most successful stanza is perhaps the last, where the connection between the dates is at once invoked as ground for some kind of mystical union and rejected as being merely fanciful:

> Fain would I feel an union with thy fate,
> Fain would I seek to draw an Omen fair
> From this connection in our Earthly date.
> Indulge the harmless weakness – Reason, spare. —

The tension here between reason and feeling touches on one of the principal concerns of eighteenth-century poetry.

Jane Austen's verses are a small and essentially private part of her work; however great her success as a novelist, in her own family it was James, not she, who was the poet. Nevertheless they reveal the mastery of style and tone familiar to us from her prose and are evidence of the importance of the family's literary pursuits in the development of her writing. For these reasons, as well as for the pleasure to be derived from them, her verses are a fascinating and revealing aspect of Jane Austen's art.

ACKNOWLEDGEMENTS

The enjoyment I have had in preparing this volume has been greatly increased by the help, advice and kindly encouragement I have received from Alwyn Austen, Tom Carpenter, David Gilson, Deirdre Le Faye, Maggie Lane, Helen Lefroy and Brian Southam; and the work has been made much easier by David Gilson's article 'Jane Austen's Verses' and Deirdre Le Faye's edition of the *Letters* and her *Jane Austen – A Family Record* (see Bibliography). I should also like to record my thanks to the following individuals, libraries and institutions: the great-grandsons of Admiral Sir Francis Austen; the descendants of Admiral Charles Austen; Jean Bowden; Anne Bradley; the Bodleian Library; the British Library; Cambridge University Library; the Centre for Kentish Studies; Ann Channon; Stephen Clewes, Bath City Council; Stephen Crook, Librarian, Berg Collection, New York Public Library; R. Custance, Fellows' Librarian, Winchester College; the East Sussex Record Office; Mark R. Farrell, Curator, Robert H. Taylor Collection, Princeton University Library; Evelyn Fowle; the Hampshire Record Office; Joan Impey; the Trustees of the Jane Austen Memorial Trust; Lorraine Jones, the Royal Pharmaceutical Society of Great Britain; Derek Lucas; John Owston, Librarian, United Oxford and Cambridge University Club; Penelope Ruddock, Bath Museums Service; Canon Walker, Winchester Cathedral; John Westmacott; Margaret Wilson.

The author and the Jane Austen Society acknowledge with gratitude the generous support of the Centre for the Study of Early English Women's Writing and the Hampshire County Council in the publication of this book.

JANE AUSTEN

Songs and verses from the Juvenilia

Jane Austen's early writings, begun when she was about thirteen, were collected by her in three notebooks which she called *Volume the First*, *Volume the Second* and *Volume the Third*. Several of these pieces, which at once reflect and parody the fiction and plays that the family read, contain short verses.

Song

That Damon was in love with me
I once thought & beleiv'd
But now that he is not I see,
I fear I was deceiv'd.

Epitaph

Here lies our freind who having promis-ed
That unto two she would be marri-ed
Threw her sweet Body & her lovely face
Into the Stream that runs thro' Portland Place.

Song

When Corydon went to the fair
He bought a red ribbon for Bess,
With which she encircled her hair
& made herself look very fess.

Song

Though misfortunes my footsteps may ever attend
  I hope I shall never have need of a Freind
as an innocent Heart I will ever preserve
  and will never from Virtue's dear boundaries swerve.

Song

Chloe]	I go to Town
	And when I come down,
	I shall be married to Stree-phon
	And that to me will be fun.
Chorus]	Be fun, be fun, be fun,
	And that to me will be fun.

    5

Song

Chloe]	I am going to have my dinner,
	After which I shan't be thinner.
	I wish I had here Strephon
	For he would carve the partridge if it should be
	a tough one.
Chorus]	Tough one, tough one, tough one,
	For he would carve the partridge if it should be
	a tough one.

    5

2

To Miss Austen, the following Ode to Pity is dedicated, from a thorough knowledge of her pitiful Nature, by her obed^t hum^{le} Servt

The Author

Ode to Pity

1

Ever musing I delight to tread
   The Paths of honour and the Myrtle Grove
Whilst the pale Moon her beams doth shed
     On disappointed Love.
While Philomel on airy hawthorn Bush   5
   Sings sweet & Melancholy, And the thrush
Converses with the Dove.

2,

Gently brawling down the turnpike road,
   Sweetly noisy falls the Silent Stream —
The Moon emerges from behind a Cloud   10
   And darts upon the Myrtle Grove her beam.
Ah! then what Lovely Scenes appear,
   The hut, the Cot, the Grot, & Chapel queer,
And eke the Abbey too a mouldering heap,
   Conceal'd by aged pines her head doth rear   15
And quite invisible doth take a peep.

'This little bag'

In January 1792 Mary Lloyd left Deane, the neighbouring parish to Steventon, when her family, who had rented the parsonage from Mr Austen, moved some sixteen miles away to Ibthorpe. Making her a present of a cotton 'housewife', or needlework bag, Jane Austen sent these verses to accompany it.

3

This little bag I hope will prove
  To be not vainly made.
For, if you thread & needle want
  It will afford you aid.

And as we are about to part   5
  T'will serve another end,
For when you look upon the Bag
  You'll recollect your Freind.

Jan:^{ry} 1792.

Lines written by Jane Austen for the amusement of a Niece,
(afterwards Lady Knatchbull) on the arrival of Captn & Mrs Austen
at Godmersham Park after their marriage July 1806

Francis Austen married Mary Gibson at Ramsgate on 24 July 1806;
Jane Austen sent these verses from Clifton to her niece Fanny at
Godmersham, where the couple were to spend the honeymoon.

See they come, post haste from Thanet,
  Lovely couple, side by side;
They've left behind them Richard Kennet
  With the Parents of the Bride!

Canterbury they have passed through;   5
  Next succeeded Stamford-bridge;
Chilham village they came fast through;
  Now they've mounted yonder ridge.

Down the hill they're swift proceeding,
  Now they skirt the Park around;   10
Lo! the Cattle sweetly feeding,
  Scamper, startled, at the sound!

4

Run, my Brothers, to the Pier gate!
    Throw it open, very wide!
Let it not be said that we're late   15
    In welcoming my Uncle's Bride!

To the house the chaise advances;
    Now it stops — They're here, they're here!
How d'ye do, my Uncle Francis?
    How does do your Lady dear?   20

'Oh! Mr Best, you're very bad'

From this poem, which is addressed 'To Martha', it is apparent that
Martha Lloyd had hoped that a certain Mr Best would escort her on
a visit to Harrogate; his lack of gallantry is teasingly rebuked, and of
course his name is a godsend.

Oh! Mr Best, you're very bad
    And all the world shall know it;
Your base behaviour shall be sung
    By me, a tuneful Poet. —

You used to go to Harrowgate   5
    Each summer as it came,
And why I pray should you refuse
    To go this year the same? —

The way's as plain, the road's as smooth,
    The Posting not increased;   10
You're scarcely stouter than you were,
    Not younger Sir at least. —

If e'er the waters were of use
    Why now their use forego?
You may not live another year,   15
    All's mortal here below. —

5

It is your duty Mr Best
  To give your health repair.
Vain else your Richard's pills will be,
  And vain your Consort's care.   20

But yet a nobler Duty calls
  You now towards the North.
Arise ennobled — as Escort
  Of Martha Lloyd stand forth.

She wants your aid — she honours you   25
  With a distinguish'd call.
Stand forth to be the friend of her
  Who is the friend of all. —

Take her, & wonder at your luck,
  In having such a Trust.   30
Her converse sensible & sweet
  Will banish heat & dust. —

So short she'll make the journey seem
  You'll bid the Chaise stand still.
T'will be like driving at full speed   35
  From Newb'ry to Speen Hill. —

Convey her safe to Morton's wife
  And I'll forget the past,
And write some verses in your praise
  As finely & as fast.   40

But if you still refuse to go
  I'll never let you rest,
But haunt you with reproachful song
  Oh! wicked Mr Best! —

                    J.A.
                Clifton 1806

On Sir Home Popham's sentence —
April 1807

The naval commander Sir Home Riggs Popham was severely reprimanded in March 1807 for having withdrawn his squadron without orders from the Cape of Good Hope.

Of a Ministry pitiful, angry, mean,
A Gallant Commander the victim is seen;
For Promptitude, Vigour, Success, does he stand
Condemn'd to receive a severe reprimand!
To his Foes I could wish a resemblance in fate;   5
That they too may suffer themselves soon or late
The Injustice they warrant — but vain is my Spite,
They cannot *so* suffer, who never do right. —

To Miss Bigg
previous to her marriage, with some pocket handfs.
I had hemmed for her. —

Cambrick! with grateful blessings would I pay
    The pleasure given me in sweat employ;
Long may'st thou serve my friend without decay,
    And have no Tears to wipe, but Tears of joy!

On the same occasion — but not sent. —

Cambrick! Thou'st been to me a Good,
And I would bless thee if I could.
Go, serve thy Mistress with delight,
Be small in compass, soft & white;
Enjoy thy fortune, honour'd much   5
To bear her name & feel her touch;
And that thy worth may last for years,
Slight be her Colds & few her Tears. —

To the Memory of Mrs Lefroy,
who died Dec:^r 16. — my Birthday. —
written 1808.

The day returns again, my natal day;
What mix'd emotions with the Thought arise!
Beloved friend, four years have pass'd away
Since thou wert snatch'd forever from our eyes.

The day, commemorative of my birth   5
Bestowing Life & Light & Hope on me,
Brings back the hour which was thy last on Earth.
Oh! bitter pang of torturing Memory!

Angelic Woman! past my power to praise
In Language meet, thy Talents, Temper, mind,   10
Thy solid Worth, thy captivating Grace! —
Thou friend & ornament of Humankind!

At Johnson's death, by Hamilton t'was said,
'Seek we a substitute — ah! vain the plan,
No second best remains to Johnson dead —   15
None can remind us even of the Man.'

So we of thee — unequall'd in thy race
Unequall'd thou, as he the first of Men.
Vainly we search around thy vacant place,
We ne'er may look upon thy like again.   20

Come then fond Fancy, thou indulgent Power, —
— Hope is desponding, chill, severe to thee! —
Bless thou, this little portion of an hour,
Let me behold her as she used to be.

I see her here, with all her smiles benign,   25
Her looks of eager Love, her accents sweet.
That voice & Countenance almost divine! —
Expression, Harmony, alike complete. —

I listen — 'tis not sound alone — 'tis sense,
'Tis Genius, Taste, & Tenderness of Soul.   30
'Tis genuine warmth of heart without pretence
And purity of Mind that crowns the whole.

She speaks; 'tis Eloquence — that grace of Tongue
So rare, so lovely! — Never misapplied
By *her* to palliate Vice, or deck a Wrong,   35
She speaks & reasons but on Virtue's side.

Her's is the Energy of Soul sincere.
Her Christian Spirit ignorant to feign,
Seeks but to comfort, heal, enlighten, chear,
Confer a pleasure, or prevent a pain. —   40

Can ought enhance such Goodness? — Yes, to me,
Her partial favour from my earliest years
Consummates all. — Ah! Give me yet to see
Her Smile of Love — the Vision disappears.

'Tis past & gone — We meet no more below.   45
Short is the Cheat of Fancy o'er the Tomb.
Oh! might I hope to equal Bliss to go!
To meet thee Angel! in thy future home!

Fain would I feel an union in thy fate,
Fain would I seek to draw an Omen fair   50
From this connection in our Earthly date.
Indulge the harmless weakness — Reason, spare. —

'Alas! poor Brag, thou boastful Game!'

The 'speaker' is the card game speculation, who commiserates with another game, brag, on their having not been played over Christmas at Godmersham.

'Alas! poor Brag, thou boastful Game! — What now avails
        thine empty name?
Where now thy more distinguish'd fame? — My day is o'er,
        & Thine the same. —
For thou like me art thrown aside, At Godmersham, this
        Christmas Tide;
And now across the Table wide, Each Game, save Brag or
        Spec: is tried.' —
'Such is the mild Ejaculation, Of tender hearted
        Speculation.' —   5

'My dearest Frank'

Francis William, the second child and eldest son of Francis and Mary Austen, was born on 12 July at Rose Cottage, outside Alton, while his father, in command of the *St Albans*, was convoying East Indiamen to China.

Copy of a letter to Frank, July 26. 1809.

My dearest Frank, I wish you joy
Of Mary's safety with a boy,
Whose birth has given little pain,
Compared with that of Mary Jane.
May he a growing Blessing prove,   5
And well deserve his Parents Love!
Endow'd with Art's & Nature's Good,
Thy name possessing with thy Blood;
In him, in all his ways, may we
Another Francis William see! —   10

Thy infant days may he inherit,
Thy warmth, nay insolence of spirit; —
We would not with one fault dispense
To weaken the resemblance.
May he revive thy Nursery sin,   15
Peeping as daringly within,
(His curley Locks but just descried)
With, 'Bet, my be not come to bide.'
Fearless of danger, braving pain,
And threaten'd very oft in vain,   20
Still may one Terror daunt his soul,
One needful engine of controul
Be found in this sublime array,
A neighbouring Donkey's aweful Bray! —
So may his equal faults as Child   25
Produce Maturity as mild.
His saucy words & fiery ways
In early Childhood's pettish days
In Manhood shew his Father's mind,
Like him considerate & kind;   30
All Gentleness to those around,
And eager only not to wound.

  Then like his Father too, he must,
To his own former struggles just,
Feel his Deserts with honest Glow,   35
And all his self-improvement know. —
A native fault may thus give birth
To the best blessing, conscious worth. —

As for ourselves, we're very well,
As unaffected prose will tell.   40
Cassandra's pen will give our state
The many comforts that await
Our Chawton home — how much we find
Already in it, to our mind,
And how convinced that when complete,   45

It will all other Houses beat
That ever have been made or mended,
With rooms concise, or rooms distended.
    You'll find us very snug next year;
Perhaps with Charles & Fanny near —   50
For now it often does delight us
To fancy them just over-right us.
                    J.A.

'In measured verse'

In the *Memoir*, the only source for this poem, we are told that Jane
Austen 'once...took it into her head to write the following mock
panegyric on a young friend, who really was clever and handsome'.
The 'young friend' is her niece Anna.

In measured verse I'll now rehearse
    The charms of lovely Anna:
And, first, her mind is unconfined
    Like any vast savannah.

Ontario's lake may fitly speak   5
    Her fancy's ample bound:
Its circuit may, on strict survey
    Five hundred miles be found.

Her wit descends on foes and friends
    Like famed Niagara's Fall;   10
And travellers gaze in wild amaze,
    And listen, one and all.

Her judgment sound, thick, black, profound,
    Like transatlantic groves,
Dispenses aid, and friendly shade   15
    To all that in it roves.

12

If thus her mind to be defined
   America exhausts,
And all that's grand in that great land
   In similes it costs —   20

Oh how can I her person try
   To image and portray?
How paint the face, the form how trace
   In which those virtues lay?

Another world must be unfurled,   25
   Another language known,
Ere tongue or sound can publish round
   Her charms of flesh and bone.

'I've a pain in my head'

In February 1811 Jane Austen went into Alton with Maria Beckford, sister-in-law of Edward Austen Knight's tenant at Chawton Great House, John Charles Middleton; Miss Beckford consulted Mr Newnham the apothecary about some 'old complaint' and this verse is supposedly their conversation 'as it actually took place'.

   'I've a pain in my head'
   Said the suffering Beckford
   To her Doctor so dread.
   'Ah! what shall I take for't.'

   Said her Doctor so dread,   5
   Whose name it was Newnham.
   'For this pain in your head,
   Ah! What can you do Ma'am?'

   Said Miss Beckford, 'Suppose
   If you think there's no risk,   10

13

I take a good Dose
Of Calomel brisk.'

'What a praise-worthy notion!'
Replied Mr Newnham
'You shall have such a potion,   15
And so will I too Ma'am.
             [Jane Austen]

On the Marriage of Mr Gell of East Bourn to Miss Gill. —

A chance reading of a newspaper announcement of the marriage of this happily named couple prompted a piece of wordplay characteristic of the Austen family (cf. James Leigh Perrot's similarly derived *On Capt. Foote's Marriage with Miss Patton*, p.52).

Of Eastbourn, Mr Gell
    From being perfectly well
Became dreadfully ill
    For the Love of Miss Gill.

So he said with some sighs
    I'm the slave of your i.s   5
Ah! restore if you please
    By accepting my e.s. —

'Between Session & Session'

Writing from Chawton to Cassandra at Godmersham on 30 April 1811, Jane Austen sent a message to her brother Edward, on the subject of the failure of a parliamentary bill in which it had been proposed to join the rivers Medway and Rother. Perhaps sensing the financial threat to toll roads posed by such new, ambitious schemes, or possibly merely out of a concern to preserve the countryside from industrialisation, he had opposed it. 'I congratulate Edward,' she wrote, 'on the Weald of Kent Canal-Bill being put off till another Session, as I have just had the pleasure of reading. There is always something to be hoped for from Delay. —' (*Letters*, p.186.)

'Between Session & Session'　　'And the villainous Bill'
'The first Prepossession'　　　'May be forced to lie still'　　5
'May rouse up the Nation'　　　'Against Wicked Men's will.'

'When stretch'd on one's bed'

The date shows this to have been written by Jane Austen three days before the appearance of her first published novel, *Sense and Sensibility*, which had originally been due out, at her own expense, in May; frustration over the delay, or anxiety as to any financial loss, may well have contributed to the occasional 'fierce-throbbing head'.

When stretch'd on one's bed
　With a fierce-throbbing head
Which precludes alike Thought or Repose,
　How little one cares
　For the grandest affairs　　　　　　5
That may busy the world as it goes! —

　How little one feels
　For the Waltzes & reels
Of our dance-loving friends at a Ball!

How slight one's concern   10
    To conjecture or learn
What their flounces or hearts may befall.

    How little one minds
    If a company dines
On the best that the Season affords!   15
    How short is one's muse
    O'er the Sauces & Stews,
Or the Guests, be they Beggars or Lords! —

    How little the Bells,
    Ring they Peels, toll they Knells   20
Can attract our attention or Ears!
    The Bride may be married,
    The Corse may be carried,
And touch nor our hopes nor our fears.

    Our own bodily pains   25
    Ev'ry faculty chains;
We can feel on no subject beside.
    'Tis in health & in Ease
    We the Power must seize
For our friends & our souls to provide.   30
            Oct.ʳ 27. 1811.
            J.A

On the marriage of Miss Camilla Wallop
& the Revᵈ [Henry] Wake.

This verse, clearly inspired by the opportunity for both a pun and a
characteristically pointed jibe at an amusingly unromantic romantic
match, refers to the engagement of a middle-aged lady, Miss Urania
Katharine Camilla Wallop, niece of the 2nd Earl of Portsmouth, to
an elderly curate, the Revd Henry Wake. They were later married at
All Saints, Southampton, 26 March 1813.

Camilla, good humoured, & merry, & small
For a Husband was at her last stake;
And having in vain danced at many a Ball
Is now happy to jump at a Wake.

Jane Austen

Written at Winchester on Tuesday the 15th July 1817

These lines on the Winchester races were written three days before
Jane Austen's death. 15 July is St Swithun's Day.

When Winchester races first took their beginning
It is said the good people forgot their old Saint
Not applying at all for the leave of St Swithin
And that William of Wykham's approval was faint.

The races however were fix'd and determin'd   5
The company met & the weather was charming
The Lords & the Ladies were sattin'd & ermin'd
And nobody saw any future alarming.

But when the old Saint was informed of these doings
He made but one spring from his shrine to the roof   10
Of the Palace which now lies so sadly in ruins
And thus he address'd them all standing aloof.

Oh, subjects rebellious, Oh Venta depraved
When once we are buried you think we are dead
But behold me Immortal. — By vice you're enslaved   15
You have sinn'd & must suffer. — Then further he said

These races & revels & dissolute measures
With which you're debasing a neighbouring Plain

17

Let them stand — you shall meet with your curse in your pleasures
Set off for your course, I'll pursue with my rain,   20

Ye cannot but know my command o'er July,
Henceforward I'll triumph in shewing my powers,
Shift your race as you will it shall never be dry
The curse upon Venta is July in showers.

J.A.

Riddles

The attributions were added to the MS in pencil, possibly, in view of
the use of the Christian name alone, by either Cassandra or one of
her brothers.

[1]

When my 1st is a task to a young girl of spirit
And my second confines her to finish the piece
How hard is her fate! but how great is her merit
If by taking my whole she effect her release!

Jane

[2]

Divided, I'm a Gentleman
In public Deeds & Powers
United, I'm a Man who oft
That Gentleman devours.

Jane

[3]

You may lie on my first, by the side of a stream,
And my second compose to the Nymph you adore
But if when you've none of my whole her esteem
And affection diminish, think of her no more.

Jane

Charade

This is Mr Elton's celebrated charade from *Emma*. For Emma's laborious explanation of it to the puzzled Harriet, see vol.1 ch.9 of that novel.

To Miss —.
Charade.

My first displays the wealth and pomp of kings,
    Lords of the earth! their luxury and ease.
Another view of man, my second brings,
    Behold him there, the monarch of the seas!

But, ah! united, what reverse we have!   5
    Man's boasted power and freedom, all are flown;
Lord of the earth and sea, he bends a slave,
    And woman, lovely woman, reigns alone.

    Thy ready wit the word will soon supply,
    May its approval beam in that soft eye!   10

FAMILY VERSE

Lines supposed to have been sent to an uncivil Dress maker —

The mourning that the dressmaker has been dilatory in making up
was for Martha Lloyd, whose mother had just died.

Miss Lloyd has now sent to Miss Green,
As, on opening the box, may be seen,
Some yards of a Black Ploughman's Gauze,
To be made up directly, because
Miss Lloyd must in mourning appear —   5
For the death of a Relative dear —
Miss Lloyd must expect to receive
This license to mourn & to grieve,
Complete, er'e the end of the week —
It is better to write than to speak —   10

                        Jane Austen

Miss Green's reply
by Mrs Austen

I've often made clothes
For those who write prose,
But 'tis the first time
I've had orders in rhyme —.
Depend on't, fair Maid,   5
You shall be obeyed;
Your garment of black
Shall sit close to your back,
And in every part
I'll exert all my art;   10

It shall be the neatest,
And eke the completest
That ever was seen —
Or my name is not Green!

Verses to rhyme with 'Rose'

The discipline imposed on these verses by the use of only one rhyme is characteristic of the kind of word-game with which the Austen family liked to amuse themselves. The authors are respectively Mrs Austen, Cassandra, Jane and Edward's wife Elizabeth Austen (later Knight – see Introduction).

Mrs *Austen*

This morning I 'woke from a quiet repose,
I first rubb'd my eyes & I next blew my nose.
With my Stockings & Shoes I then cover'd my toes
And proceeded to put on the rest of my Cloathes.
This was finish'd in less than an hour I suppose;   5
I employ'd myself next in repairing my hose
'Twas a work of necessity, not what I chose;
Of my sock I'd much rather have knit twenty Rows. —
My work being done, I looked through the win*dows*
And with pleasure beheld all the Bucks & the Does,   10
The Cows & the Bullocks, the Wethers & Ewes. —
To the Lib'ry each morn, all the Family goes,
So I went with the rest, though I felt rather froze.
My flesh is much warmer, my blood freer flows
When I work in the garden with rakes & with hoes.   15
And now I beleive I must come to a close,
For I find I grow stupid e'en while I compose;
If I write any longer my verse will be prose.

Miss Austen

Love, they say is like a Rose;
I'm sure tis like the wind that blows,
For not a human creature knows
How it comes or where it goes.
It is the cause of many woes,   5
It swells the eyes & reds the nose,
And very often changes those
Who once were friends to bitter foes.
But let us now the scene transpose
And think no more of tears & throes.   10
Why may we not as well suppose
A smiling face the Urchin shows?
And when with joy: the Bosom glows,
And when the heart has full repose,
'Tis Mutual Love the gift bestows. —   15

Miss J. Austen

Happy the Lab'rer in his Sunday Cloathes! —
In light-drab coat, smart waistcoat, well-darn'd Hose
And hat upon his head to Church he goes; —
As oft with conscious pride he downward throws
A glance upon the ample Cabbage rose   5
Which stuck in Buttonhole regales his nose,
He envies not the gayest London Beaux. —
In Church he takes his seat among the rows,
Pays to the Place the reverence he owes,
Likes best the Prayers whose meaning least he knows,   10
Lists to the Sermon in a softening Doze,
And rouses joyous at the welcome close. —

Never before did I quarrel with a Rose
Till now that I am told some lines to compose,
Of which I shall have little idea God knows! —
But since that the Task is assign'd me by those
To whom Love, Affection & Gratitude owes   5
A ready compliance, I feign would dispose
And call to befriend me the Muse who bestows
The gift of Poetry both on Friends & Foes. —
My warmest acknowledgements are due to those
Who watched near my Bed & soothed me to repose   10
Who pitied my sufferings & shared in my woes,
And by their simpathy relieved my sorrows.
May I as long as the Blood in my veins flows
Feal the warmth of Love which now in my heart glows,
And may I sink into a refreshing Doze   15
When I lie my head on my welcome pillows.

Bouts-Rimés
(Written at Chawton Cottage, 1820)

In this word-game, originating from France, the players had to write
verses on a list of rhymed words, keeping to the given order. These
examples are by Mrs Austen (the initials standing for 'Cassandra
Austen') and her grandson George Knight.

Words given — *Verse — Sorrow — Hearse — Purse — Morrow.*

Why d'you ask me to scribble in verse
When my heart's full of trouble and sorrow?
The cause I will briefly rehearse,
I'm in debt, with a sad empty purse,
And the bailiffs will seize me to-morrow.   5

C.A.

I've said it in prose, and I'll say it in verse,
That riches bring comfort and poverty sorrow,
That it's better to ride in a coach than a hearse,
That it's better to fill than to empty your purse,
And to feast well to-day than to fast till to-morrow.   5
                              C.A.

                    To mutton I am not averse,
                        But veal I eat with sorrow,
                    So from my cradle to my hearse
                    For calves I'd never draw my purse,
                        For lambs I would to-morrow.   5
                              G.K.

I hate your French tragedies written in verse,
    They fill me with laughter, not sorrow;
What Racine has written, let Talma rehearse,
The notions I've formed he would never disperse,
    Though he laboured fron now till to-morrow.   5
                              G.K.

MRS AUSTEN

Steventon 1779

Epistle to G. East Esqr

Gilbert East (1764-1828), son of Sir William East of Hall Place,
Hurley, Berkshire, was one of four pupils of Mr Austen living at
Steventon rectory, to be educated alongside his own sons Edward
and Henry. During a prolonged absence from his studies these
verses were written for him.

Your Steventon Friends
Are at their wits ends
To know what has become of Squire East;
They very much fear
He'll never come here   5
Having left them nine weeks at the least.

Two letters he sent
In hopes to prevent
Or lessen their wonder & trouble;
But as he still stays,   10
And creates fresh delays
Instead of being less, it is double.

Then pray thee, dear Sir,
No longer defer
Your return to the mansion of learning;   15
For we study all day,
(Except when we play)
And eke when the candles are burning —

Of Dan: Virgil we say
Two lessons each day;   20
The story is quite entertaining;

25

You have lost the best part,
But come, take a good heart,
Tho' we've read six, there are six books remaining

But we're somewhat afraid   25
Now so long you have stay'd
That all your poor books are forsaken;
And not e'en a Romance
Now stands the least chance
From your book case of ever being taken.   30

That 'Cassandra' herself
May now lie on your shelf
No longer affording you pleasure;
While new tunes & new dances
And such pretty fancies   35
Employ all your thoughts & your leisure.

That such things as these
May delight, & may please
We do not pretend to deny;
But it's not quite so clever   40
To be dancing for ever
And let all your learning lie by

That you dance very well
All beholders can tell,
For lightly & nimbly you tread;   45
Bu, pray, is it meet
To indulge thus your feet
And neglect all the while y^r poor head?

So we send you this letter
In hopes you'll think better,   50
And reflect upon what we have said;
And to make us amends
Pray return to your Friends,
Fowle, Stewart, Deane, Henry, & Ned!

To F.S. *who accused the Author of partiality in writing verses for F C Fowle, & not for him.*

This verse is addressed to Frank Stuart, one of Mr Austen's pupils.

Ah! why Friend Frank
D'ye look so blank,
So wondrous discontented?
Each lucky hit,
Each stroke of wit,   5
Are by those looks prevented.

The cheerful Muse
Does here refuse
To lend her kind assistance;
She cannot bear   10
A serious air,
So wisely keeps her distance

Yet I must write
This very night,
Or you will look still graver;   15
And I shall be
Reproached by Thee
That rhyming goes by favour.

But oh dismiss
A thought like this,   20
Which does me such injustice;
I mind always
That rule which says
'Serve that Man first who first is.'

And now, my Friend,   25
I pray unbend
That brow so long contracted;

And never break
(For your own sake)
The following law enacted.   30

I here decree
That you nor he
Shall ever be offended;
Or e're be wont
To take affront   35
Where no affront's intended —

The humble petition of R^d Buller & W. Goodenough

A somewhat unusual complaint from two of the rectory pupils is
turned by Mrs Austen into a petition on their behalf to her husband.

Dear Sir, We beseech & intreat & request
You'd remove a sad nuisance that breaks our night's rest
That creaking old weathercock over our heads
Will scarcely permit us to sleep in our beds.
It whines & it groans & makes such a noise   5
That it greatly disturbs two unfortunate boys
Who hope you will not be displeased when they say
If they don't sleep by night they can't study by day.
But if you will kindly grant this their petition
And they sleep all night long without intermission   10
They promise to study hard every day
And moreover as bounden in duty will pray etc., etc.

'I send you here'

Assemblies were held in the Town Hall at Basingstoke; the Austens
and their friends were regular attenders.

Steventon 1794

I send you here a list of all
The company who graced the Ball
Last Thursday night at Basingstoke;
There were but six & thirty folk,
Although the evening was so fine;   5
First then, the couple from the Vine, —
Next Squire Hicks, & his fair spouse;
They came from Mr Bramston's house,
With Madam, & her maiden Sister;
(Had she been absent who'd have missed her?)   10
And fair Miss Woodward, that sweet singer,
For Mrs Bramston liked to bring her.
With Alethea too, & Harriet;
They came in Mrs Hicks's chariot;
Perhaps they did, I am not certain.   15
Then there were 4 good folk from Worting:
For with the Clerks there came two more;
Some friends of their's, their name was Hoare.
With M^r M^{rs}, Miss Lefroy
Came Henry Rice, that pleasant Boy.   20
And least a title they should want,
There came Sir Colebrook, & Sir Grant
Miss Eyre of Sherfield, & her Mother;
One Miss from Dummer, & her Brother.
    Her Mother too, as Chaperon.   25
    M^r & Mrs Williamson.
Charles Powlett, & his Pupils twain:
Small Parson Hasker, great Squire Lane.
And Bentworth's Rector, with his hat,
Unwillingly he parts from that.   30

29

Two Misses Davies, with two friends;
And thus my information ends.

P.S.   It would have been a better dance
          But for the following circumstance;
          The Dorchesters, so high in station,   35
          Dined out that day, by invitation,
          At Heckfield Heath, with Squire Le Fevre;
          Methinks it was not quite so clever
          For one Subscriber to invite
          Another, on the assembly night;   40
          But 'twas to meet a General Donne
          His Lordship's old companion;
          And as the General would not stay
          They could not fix another day —

Dialogue between Death and M^{rs} A:

Early in 1804, when the Austens were living at 4 Sydney Place, Bath, Mrs Austen was very ill, and was treated by the apothecary, Mr Bowen.

   Says Death 'I've been trying these three weeks or more
To seize on Old Madam here at number four,
Yet I still try in vain, tho she's turn'd of threescore,
To what is my ill success oweing'?
I'll tell you, old Fellow, if you cannot guess,   5
To what you're indebted for your ill success;
To the Prayers of my Husband, whose love I possess,
To the care of my Daughters, whom Heaven will bless;
To the skill and attention of BOWEN.

Fables

In these three versifications of Æsop Mrs Austen takes as her model the popular verse Fables by John Gay, many of which were printed in *Elegant Extracts* (see Introduction).

1

A Cock was working very hard
Upon a Dunghill in the Yard,
The morn was sharp, his hunger keen,
He scratch'd & scratch'd & scratch'd again;
At length a precious Stone he found,   5
(T'was worth at least a hundred pound)
Thou art a mere glittering Toy, says he,
Not of the smallest use to me,
To man thy value may be great,
I had rather find a grain of Wheat!   10

2

Some fine ripe Grapes were hanging high,
A hungry Fox was passing by,
He lick'd his lips & long'd to eat 'em,
So Jump'd & Jump'd but could not get 'em;
Convinced it was not in his power,   5
I'm sure, said he, those Grapes are sour.

3

A country man, who, I am told
Is nearly ninety-nine years old,
One morn, the weather being good,
Crept to the Copse to pick up wood,
And, having got his little load,   5
Came slowly back along the road;
But e'er he half the way had got
The sun shone bright, the day grew hot,

31

Quite tired & almost out of breath,
He sat him down & call'd for Death: 10
Death came, & ask'd him what he'd have,
'Sir, I would your assistance crave,
I flung my Faggot down thro' pain,
Pray help me get it up again'.

A receipt for a Pudding

This was contributed to the book of recipes compiled by Martha
Lloyd at Chawton, *c*. 1808.

If the vicar you treat,
You must give him to eat,
A pudding to hit his affection;
And to make his repast,
By the canon of taste,   5
Be the present receipt your direction.

first take two pounds of Bread,
Be the crumb only weigh'd,
For crust the good house-wife refuses;
The proportion you'll guess,   10
May be made more or less,
To the size that each family chuses.

Then its sweetness to make
Some currants you take
And Sugar of each half a pound   15
Be not butter forgot
And the quantity sought
Must the same with your currants be found

Cloves & mace you will want,
With rose water I grant,   20
And more savory things if well chosen;
Then to bind each ingredient,
You'll find it expedient,
Of Eggs to put in half a dozen.

Some milk dont refuse it,   25
But boiled ere you use it,
A proper hint this for its maker;
And the whole when compleat,
In a pan clean and neat,
With care recommend to the baker.   30

In praise of this pudding,
I vouch it a good one,
Or should you suspect a fond word;
To every Guest,
Perhaps it is best,   35
Two puddings should smoke on the board.

Two puddings! — yet — no,
For if one will do,
The other comes in out of season;
And these lines but obey,   40
Nor can anyone say,
That this pudding's with-out rhyme or reason

'I hope, my Anna'

These congratulatory lines were sent by Mrs Austen to her grand-daughter Anna Austen on the day after her marriage to Ben Lefroy.

I hope, my Anna, you'll believe
Of all the Letters you receive
None contain wishes more sincere
Than these I send to you, my dear;
To you, but not to you alone,   5
My Grandson shares in every one.
I wish you happiness and health,
I wish you an increase of wealth,
(Id make you richer if I could)
I wish you every kind of good.   10
But ills attend us from our birth,
And will, while we remain on Earth.
You must not look for perfect bliss,
That's for a better life than this;
But may your troubles here be small,   15
Your comforts great. — And when the call
Of our Creator takes you hence,
May you receive a recompence
For each good act, good word, good thought,
Pardon for each repented fault;   20
And then, in heavenly mansions, be
Most bless'd to all Eternity.
       Chawton, Wednesday Novr 9th 1814

Riddles and Charades

1

Say, what am I? or what are we?
For I am more than one,
I never speak, I cannot see,
I've neither flesh or bone.

In England I have ne'er been seen,   5
And think I never shall;
In Wales, where I have always been,
M'importance is not small;

For there I lead a chosen few,
Who all in black appear,   10
One's rather crooked it is true,
And One's a grenadier.

In wintery weather, windy, wet,
I never quit my place.
Foremost in war, and never yet   15
Been in the least disgrace.

Altho so brave, I'm poor & old,
In wrinkles and in want,
Tis true I feel nor heat nor cold,
And be in pain — I can't.   20

But tho not hot, I'm in a sweat,
Yet garments I wear never.
I'm in the Law, but nothing get,
I'm in the wrong for ever.

In a weak way I long have been,   25
Yet own no habitation,
Tho in the window I am seen,
Of each house in the nation —.

Riddle 2^d

I have a mouth, but never eat,
My food being rather drink than meat,
   Which never makes me ill,
Altho' it does not with me stay,
In truth I vomit twice a day,   5
   Yet I keep drinking still

The Kitchen is my proper place,
And there I shew a dirty face,
   And am a nasty creature;
But when I in the parlour come,   10
Or in the nicer drawing-room,
   I then look smart & neater.

I never speak, but often sing,
Which does both hope & pleasure bring
   And raises expectation;   15
I sing till I can sing no more,
But when my harmony is o'er
   Am in great agitation.

I have my faults, (for who has not?)
I own I'm often very hot,   20
   But I'm of worse accused;
They'll tell you I am scandal's friend,
But do not to such tales attend,
   Believe me, I'm abused.

Riddle 3^d

That you will quickly find me out
I own I have but little doubt,
For, if you please to make enquiry,
You'll find me in the Ladies Diary.
Would you my residence discover?   5
Look for me in the Town of Dover,

Most likely you will find me there,
Tho I've a place in Dorsetshire;
The Country's fine & dry & pleasant
Well stock'd with Foxes, Hare & Pheasant,   10
But these to me afford no fruit,
I never hunt, and cannot shoot;
But you'll suppose me happy there
On those fine Downs to breathe fine Air?
But no such pleasures I possess,   15
I am in debt and deep distress;
I never wish to see a stranger,
For I am constantly in danger;
He who has Bailiffs in his head
Like me, must always be in dread;   20
For who wou'd like, in Jail, to be
Depriv'd of his sweet liberty?
Then say, if such a life of Woe
Be worth the having, surely no.
Well then, no longer I'll survive —   25
But stop — I've never been alive,
I never walk'd, I never spoke,
What then, is all you've said a Joke?
No, every Syllable is true —
I only mean to puzzle you.   30

Riddle [4]

I've a circular form, but I've never a head,
I am usually Black 'tho sometimes I am red.
I have several companions of Various Shapes,
Some tall and well form'd, some ugly as Apes.
Tho I really can't boast of e'er earning a penny,   5
With the help of a comrade I've fleeced a great Many
But it did me no good, I'm in poverty still,
And so must remain, let me do what I will.
Tho I never was married I'm always in love
And I still am in hopes; How falacious they prove!   10

37

I'm of great use in Oxford, that Fountain of Knowledge,
And a place is found for me in every College.
Tho with Knowledge or Learning, I'm very ill stored
Without my assistance you can't write a Word.

Riddle [5]
Two Letters form me while I've Breath
When kill'd, I've need of Four,
But if I die a natural Death
Must have Three Letters more

[6]
Sometimes I am bright, sometimes covered with soot
I'm of very great use at a feast,
I am often applied to the right or left foot
I'm a Fish, I'm a Boy, I'm a beast

C.A. Sen[r]

[7]
My 1st when good may claim another
My 2[d] Water cannot smother
My whole stands in the way before ye
And puts a stop to speed & hurry

C.A. Sen[r]

[8]
My 1st implied Mirth, & my 2[d] reflection
If my whole you divide in a proper direction
It will tell you your fortune, & answer your question.

C.A. sen[r]

[9]

My first's a handsome horned beast
And so indeed's my second;
My whole is manufactured goods
    Not fit for garments reckoned
'Tis smooth & strong & somewhat stiff   5
    And not so fine as chintz
Yet our old Poet Shakespear says
    't'was once worn by a Prince.

                                    C.A.
                                        Sen[r]

JAMES AUSTEN

Epilogue to the Sultan
a farce acted at Steventon Jany 1790
spoken by Miss Cooper as Roxalana

In *The Sultan* by Isaac Bickerstaffe (1775) the heroine, a lively English
girl, sees off the entire harem and becomes sole empress.

Lord help us! What strange foolish things are these men
One good clever woman is fairly worth ten!
For though the vain creatures will talk by the hour
Of Woman's submission & Man's sov'reign power,
Yet we know by experience that best of all rules   5
That the wisest of men have by us been made fools;
That how e're for a while they may bluster and storm,
They will all in the end to our wishes conform.
Do you doubt? Only watch all y^r friends who are married
And see by whose will house-hold matters are carried   10
And you'll find in all ranks all conditions & stations
(At least amongst polished & civilized nations)
From the Dame who in wedlock ten years has been tried
To the Lass who has only ten months been a bride
That by open command or insidious direction   15
My lady has got the good man in subjection.
And though to all *force* to submit he refuses,
To *oblige her* he commonly does what she chuses.
'My Dear I'm going out.' 'Going out my Love! Where?'
'Only just for a walk as the evening is fair;'   20
Nay indeed you shall tell me, I must & will know;'
'Why I'm going to the club.' 'I declare you shant go,
'To the club with your cold! In such weather as this!
'I'm sure for this once you may very well miss;
'And you know the last meeting you made it so late   25
'There four tedious hours at home did I wait —
'Not at home till past ten, but if men can but roam,

40

'They ne'er mind what their families suffer at home.
'But you surely wo'nt go —' 'Why if you Ma'am refuse
'Your permission, I suppose I *must* send an excuse.'   30
'My permission! I see you have misunderstood —
'I refuse! I am sure I but spoke for your good.
'A wife's my aversion her husband who teazes —
'And I beg my dear Love will do just as he pleases'
'Nay my Dear if you really — I believe you are right,   35
'It is as you say a most terrible night.'
'Then you will stay at home to night, wont you? say yes'⎫
'Yes.' 'There I thought so, come give me a kiss,   ⎬
'You ca'nt think dear good man how I love you for this.'⎭
Thus also, but Lord what a mad cap am I,   40
Who have tried into secrets forbidden to pry!
Who in hopes, perhaps vain, of our audience diverting
Have dared to peep behind the connubial curtain.
Yet believe me, though wildly I rattle to night,
I am yet, & with reason enough in a fright;   45
For though I've been able by various expedients,
To reduce a proud Turk to true Christian obedience;
Though the Mufti, The Vizier, the Aga I've spurned,
And an Empire's fixed laws by a laugh overturned,
Yet vain the endeavour my fears to repress,   50
When this solemn Divan I a suppliant address,
To beg they'll accept our acknowledgments hearty
For the honor they've done our theatrical party;
That they'll pass without censure our faults & omissions
And try to be pleased with our light exhibitions,   55
That they'll cheerfully take what was honestly meant,
Our failures forgive, & applaud our intent —

To Edward on the death of his first pony

James Edward was the third of James Austen's four children; he was twelve years old when this poem was written.

'Why weeps my Boy?' His Father said;
Poor Edward points to Pony dead;
'And see,' with trembling voice he cries,
'How stiff his limbs, how glazed his eyes;
Yes, my poor humble faithful friend,   5
'Thy life has reached its' destined end.
'Ne'er shall I more at early day,   ⎫
'As to thy stall I take my way,   ⎬
'Hear thy light, chearful, welcome neigh: ⎭
'No more at evening or at morn,   10
'Thy manger fill with sifted corn;
'Fresh sain foin put within thy rack,
'Kiss thy soft cheek or pat thy back.
'No more, as in the dewy mead
'I turn thee unconfined to feed,   15
'View thee with saucy boldness run,
'John's proffered sieve & halter shewn,
'Yet quiet stand when I come near
'And let me catch thee void of fear.
'No more, as on thy back I ride,   20
'Mark they quick step with conscious pride,
'Thy steps which scarcely print the grass,
'And many a taller pony pass.
'With secret pleasure view the gaze
'Of travellers in the rapid chaise,   25
'And er'e their wonder words can find
'Leave them almost a mile behind.
'These joys are flown, they come no more,
'And long must I thy loss deplore;
'Nor, while I live, expect to see   30
'A favourite I can love like thee;

'Take then, my darling pony, this
'My last farewell, my parting kiss.

He spoke, & bending o'er the corse
Kissed the last time his favourite horse,   35
Then slowly turned, & with a look,
Which mingled grief & love bespoke,
His Father's hand in silence took.

That hand his Father fondly pressed
And thus his weeping boy addressed.   40
'Think not I blame your tears my Love,
'Pleased I behold your conduct prove
'By grief so pure, so void of art,
'That you possess a feeling heart;
'Tis the first loss you ever knew;   45
'A greater trial far to you,
'Than they can tell, who often crossed
'By Life's maturer ills have lost
'What nothing ever can regain,
'Youth's kindly sense of joy & pain.   50
'Yet check awhile this burst of grief,
'Let reason come to your relief.
      'In every woe at every age,
'Which meets us in life's bustling stage
'The ills which on ourselves we bring   55
'Alone can have a lasting sting.
'Say, had you e'er your power abused,
'Had you your Pony harshly used,
'Had you with cruel spur & thong
'Driven the poor tried wretch along,   60
'Or, when oppressed with labour hard,
'Left him to shiver in the yard,
'Ne'er seen him littered, rubbed, or fed,
'How would you bear to see him dead?
'How bitter then would be the thought   65
'You had not used him as you ought
'But you can view, nor conscience blame,

43

'(And may you ever do the same)
'Your conduct to your little steed,
'For sure I am no Quadrupede   70
'A kinder milder master knew
'Than Pony ever found in you.
'Then let this thought your bosom cheer,
'Check the deep sigh, & flowing tear,
'And from this loss your mind prepare   75
'More serious ills of life to bear.

    'Happy as yet your days have flown,
'More joys than sorrows you have known,
'But do not think, my dearest Boy,
'Life is a scene of unmixed joy.   80
'Your comforts always to retain
'Were hope alas! absurd & vain:
'Each blessing that you now possess
'Time's lapse itself will soon make less;
'And, if you live, you'll live to mourn   85
'Full many joys that ne'r return.
'Around you now collected see
'Relations, friends, & family;
'Within a constant circle move,
'Endeared by bonds of mutual love;   90
'Yet these must all, (nay do not start,)
'From you, and from each other part;
'The time will come, when every year
'Takes from you some one you hold dear.
'Oh! then, as now, may no remorse   95
'Increase affliction's native force;
'No vain regrets for joys abused,
'Neglected friends, & time misused,
'Imprint a sorrow in your breast
'More hard to bear than all the rest.   100
'May the light woes of early youth
'Teach you this salutary truth;
'That every sorrow will be light,
'When all within our breasts is right;

44

'That a well regulated mind   105
'In such distress will comfort find,
'And, unreproving Conscience still
'Provide a cure for every ill,
                                        Jany 1811.

Tyger's letter to Caroline   1812

This verse, supposedly written by the rectory cat to his young
mistress, together with the 'Address to Tyger', below, show James
Austen at his most playful, and also perhaps his most skilful.

Ever honoured Mistress mine,
Condescend to read a line
Written by my little paws,
And defend poor Tyger's cause.
    Wicked Harriet has said   5
Tyger heavy made the bread;
Believe her not; 'tis all a lie,
Harriet spoilt the bread, not I.
Very true it is, I know,
I slept a little on the dough;   10
But surely that could do no harm;
No, no, 'twas Betsey up at Farm
Sent her down some shocking barm.
    Or else Harriet had been drinking,
Or upon her sweetheart thinking,   15
And did not knead the dough enough,
And when she found her bread was tough
Laid it on Tyger in a huff.
Tell her a shame it is that she
Should lay her careless faults on me,   20
And that I'll make her rue the day
If she again the same should say.
For, should I see a hundred mice

Eating up her tartlets nice,
I will not interrupt their fun,   25
I will not catch a single one.
Hence forth for me, both rat & mouse
Shall unmolested haunt the house,
Shall run about where er'e they please
And nibble bread & meat & cheese.   30
    Nay more, when Harriet goes to bed
The mice shall frisk about her head,
And when she tries her eyes to close
A rat shall bite her by the nose.
Besides, I'll tell you what I'll do,   35
Close at her door all night I'll mew
And such a dismal wailing keep
She shall not get a wink of sleep,
Shall lose her rest, & health, & fat
Because she blamed a harmless cat.   40

                                        Tyger

Address to Tyger
*on his stealing the steak reserved for
the author's luncheo[n].*

Sure you are Tyger rightly named,
A savage never to be tamed,
Of disposition wild and rude;
Yes, monster of ingratitude,
Come forth, & answer for yourself;   5
What made you climb upon the shelf,
And with remorseless labour take
My next day's meal, my mutton steak?
    Let all the world now judge between us;
Yes, you're a very fine Micænas,   10
Thus with fresh hunger to reward
The verses of a hungry Bard!

Who, when you slept upon the dough,
(Dont shake your tail, tis true you know)
Stood forth your champion, and took   15
Your part against the angry cook?
But he no more your part will take
Since this is the return you make.
What could induce you, much I wonder,
To this audacious act of plunder?   20
'Twas not by hunger you were wrought
For you are better fed than taught.
Your little mistress sees to that,
She ne'er neglects her favourite cat.
It was not mere retaliation;   25
I never gave you provocation;
I ne'er purloined a bit of fat
From a cold boiled or roasted rat;
And can aver with conscience clear
I have not ate a mouse this year.   30
No, 'twas an act of wanton spite,
Or else of guttling appetite.
And now I have your crime depicted,
I hope that you stand self convicted;
And will not purr a single word   35
Untill your sentence you have heard.
        I pardon this your first offence,
And trust you have a proper sense
Of sorrow, & bewail your guilt
And mourn the gravy you have spilt.   40
But should you hence forth ever more
Be caught within the pantry door,
You then to *Corbet's* shall be sent,
(Where for her crimes your sister went)
And he shall shoot you through the head,   45
And strip your skin off when you're dead,
And there your fur as soft as ermine,
Shall hang midst mean & vulgar vermin;
Midst stoats & weazels shall have place,

A lesson to the tabby race;   50
That future cats may warning take
Nor dare to steal a mutton steak.
                    Decr 1812.

'Venta! within thy sacred fane'

James Austen was himself in failing health at the time of his sister's
death in 1817 and he was unable to attend her funeral, which took
place in Winchester Cathedral on 24 July.

Venta! within thy sacred fane
Rests many a chief in battle slain;
And many a Statesman great & wise
Beneath thy hallowed pavement lies:
Tracing thy venerable pile,   5
Thy Gothic choir and Pillared Aisle;
Frequent we tread the vaulted grave
Where sleep the learned & the Brave.
High on the Screen on either hand
Old Saxons Monarchs Coffins stand.   10
Below beneath his sable Stone
Lies the Conquerors haughty Son;
Immured within the Chapels wall
Sleep Mitred Priest and Cardinal.
And honoured Wickham lies reclined   15
In Gothic tracery enshrined.

    But sure since Williams purer taste
Old Walkelyn's heavier style effaced
Ore the plain roof the fret work spread
And formed the Arch with lancet head;   20
Neer did this venerable fane
More Beauty, Sense & worth contain
Than when upon a Sister's bier
Her Brothers dropt the bitter tear.

48

In her (rare union) were combined   25
A fair form and a fairer mind
Hers, Fancy quick, and clear good sense
And wit which never gave offence:
A Heart as warm as ever beat,
A Temper even calm and sweet: 30
Though quick and keen her mental eye
Poor natures foibles to descry
And seemed for ever on the watch
Some traits of ridicule to catch.
Yet not a word she ever pen'd   35
Which hurt the feelings of a friend
And not a line she ever wrote
'Which dying, she would wish to blot.'
    But to her family alone
Her real & genuine worth was known: 40
Yes! They whose lot it was to prove
Her Sisterly, her Filial love,
They saw her ready still to share
The labours of domestic care
As if their prejudice to shame;   45
Who jealous of fair female fame
Maintain, that literary taste
In womans mind is much displaced;
Inflames their vanity and pride,
And draws from useful works aside.   50

Such wert Thou, Sister! whilst below
In this mixt scene of joy and woe,
To have thee with us it was given
A special kind behest of Heaven.
What *now* thou art! we cannot tell: 55
Nor where, the just made perfect dwell
Know we as yet: to us denied
To draw that parting veil aside,
Which twixt two different worlds outspread
Divides the Living from the Dead.   60

But yet with all humility,
The change, we trust was [fair] for thee.
For oh! If so much genuine worth
In its imperfect state on Earth
So fair and so attractive proved   65
By all around admired and loved:
Who then the Change dare calculate
Attendant on that happy state,
When by the body unconfined
All Sense, Intelligence and mind   70
By Seraphs born through realms of light
(While Angles gladden at the sight)
The Atherial Spirit wings its way
To regions of attendant day. —

To Miss Jane Austen the reputed Author of Sense and Sensibility a Novel lately publish'd

This poem, in a disguised hand, was sent in the form of a letter, presumably in 1811; it bears a very ornate inscription to 'Miss Jane Austen' and the Alton postmark. For the attribution to James Austen see the textual note, p.74.

On such Subjects no Wonder that she shou'd write well,
In whom so united those Qualities dwell;
Where 'dear Sensibility', Sterne's darling Maid,
With Sense so attemper'd is finely pourtray'd.
Fair Elinor's Self in that Mind is exprest,   5
And the Feelings of Marianne live in that Breast.
Oh then, gentle Lady! continue to write,
And the Sense of your Readers t'amuse & delight.
                                        A Friend.

Charade

In my first that he may not be tardy & late
My second to do & make nobody wait
A curate oft crosses the plain
But if to my whole he sh^d ever advance
To me it appears an improbable chance   5
That he'll ever do either again.

                JA.

JAMES LEIGH PERROT

On Capt. Foote's Marriage with Miss Patton

The attribution to James Leigh Perrot is made in the *Memoir*. The marriage took place on 24 August 1803.

Thro' the rough ways of Life, with a patten on your Guard,
    May you safely and pleasantly jog;
May the ring never break, nor the Knot press too hard,
    Nor the Foot find the Patten a Clog.

Riddles

[1]

Two brothers wisely kept apart, together are employ'd
Tho' to one purpose both are bent, each takes a different side.
To us nor heads nor mouths belong; yet plain our tongues appear
With them we never speak a word, without them useless are
In blood, & wounds we deal, yet good in temper we are proved   5
We are from passion always free yet oft in anger moved
We travel much, yet prisoners are, & close confined to boot
Can with the swiftest horse keep pace, yet always go on foot
                                                        JLP.

[2]

In confinement I'm chained every day
    Yet my enemies need not be crowing
To my chain I have always a key
    And no prison can keep me from going
Small & weak are my hands I allow   5
    Yet for striking my character's great
Tho' ruined by one fatal blow

52

My strokes if hard prest, I repeat.
I have neither mouth eye nor ear
 Yet I always keep time as I sing   10
Change of seasons I never need fear
 Tho' my being depends on the spring.
Would you wish if these hints are too few
 One glimpse of my figure to catch
Look round; I shall soon be in view   15
 If you have but your eyes on the watch
        JLP.

[3]

Each day by the Clown I'm employed.
Each day by the King am I placed.
Few at court are more polished than I
Yet I'm oft for my bluntness disgraced.
That the edge of his appetite's gone   5
The dram drinking toper may cry
But a whet every morning mends mine
And more sharp set for dinner am I.
Each morn I grow thinner & thinner,
This custom must shorten my days   10
But why need I fear its effects
While each night I am still in good case.
If too near I approach you, beware
Or mischief perhaps may ensue;
But closely if once you can clasp me   15
No mischief can happen to you.
My point is to help all my friends
And yet such a queer blade am I,
That if I but give you the slip
To catch me — 'tis folly to try —   20
        JLP.

CASSANDRA ELIZABETH AUSTEN

Charades

[1]

Should you chance to suffer thirst
Turn my second to my first
My whole is in the garden dug
And may be fairly called a drug
C.E.A.

[2]

My 1st is a hindrance, my 2^{d} a snare
With nothing between them I boldly declare;
My whole is a title, sometimes the reward
Of Value, or Science, but it is not a Lord.
C.E.A.

FRANCIS WILLIAM AUSTEN

Charade

By my 1st you may travel with safety & speed
Though many dislike the conveyance indeed.
My 2^{d} no woman can well be
My whole takes a change several times in each year
Hot, & cold, wet & dry, benignant severe
What am I, fair Lady, pray tell me
F.W.A.

5

CHARLES JOHN AUSTEN

Charade

In *Charades etc Written a hundred years ago By Jane Austen and Her Family* this is wrongly attributed to the Revd George Austen; it was actually written by his youngest son, Charles John Austen.

Without me divided, fair ladies I ween
At a ball or a concert you'll never be seen
You must do me together or safely I'd swear
Whatever your carriage you'd never get there
                                    CJA.

HENRY THOMAS AUSTEN

Charade

I with a Housemaid once was curst
Whose name when shortened makes my first;
She an ill natured Jade was reckoned
And in the house oft raised my second
My whole stands high in lists of fame   5
Exalting e'en great Chatham's name.
                                    H.T.A.

Godmersham
The Temple of Delight

The stock phraseology of Henry Austen's encomium to his brother Edward's house, no doubt left there after a visit, is turned into a gleeful parody by his young nephew, George Knight, in the verse which follows it.

Gentle Pilgrim, rest thy feet,
Open is the gate to thee;
Do not doubt that thou shalt meet
   Mirth and Hospitality.
Elegance & grace shall charm thee,   5
Reason shall with wit unite —
Sterling sense shall here inform thee
How domestic love can find
All the blessings, which combined
Make the Temple of Delight.   10
              H.T. Austen

GEORGE KNIGHT

George Knight to his Dog Pincher

Gentle Pincher, cock thy tail,
   Open is the door to thee;
Enter, & there ne'er shall fail
   Mirth & Hospitality —
Partridge bones, & Pork shall charm thee   5
   Mutton shall with Veal unite;
Sterling Beef shall then inform thee
   How domestic Dogs can find
   All the savings, which combined
   Make the Temple of Delight —   10

JANE ANNA ELIZABETH AUSTEN
(ANNA LEFROY)

On reading a letter

The letter was from the Revd Michael Terry, with whom Anna Austen had entered into an engagement strongly disapproved of by her family (see 'In measured verse', p.12). Like Fanny Knight's poem, below, this was written during a visit by Anna to Godmersham in 1809-10.

With what delight I view each line
Trac'd by the hand I love
Where warm esteem & Grace combine
A feeling heart to move

2

Then come sweet letter to my breast   5
Thoul't find no coldness there
Close to my heart for ever rest
It's warmth for ever share —
                    J.A.E. Austen
                    Dec.ᵇʳ 1809

FANNY KNIGHT

To Anna Eliza Austen

This Year is done
Its course is run
Its pleasures & its pains
Alike are o'er
And they no more   5
Shall fill our anxious brains.

But may I ask
Who can the task
Of introspection bear?
    And turn their eye   10
    Without a sigh
Back on the closing Year?

    Anna can you
    Look back & view
This checquered scene of Woes   15
    And not lament
    The short time spent
In thinking of its close?
                F.C. Austen
                Dec^{br} 31st
                1809

JAMES EDWARD AUSTEN-LEIGH

Lines addressed to his Father
on making him a present of a knife —

This is a letter addressed to the Revd James Austen at Steventon; it
has no date, though the paper has a watermark of 1810, when James
Edward was twelve. Since it accompanied the gift of a knife, it was
presumably given by hand.

My dear Papa
    Though superstitious Folks may say
    That if a Knife you give away,
    T'will cut the love of Friends most true, ⎫
    Yet I feel sure I ne'er shall rue   ⎬
    The Day I gave this Knife to you;   ⎭   5
    For I am certain that no steel
    Can hurt the love which I shall feel

For ever for my Parent dear,
Therefore my Father do not fear
This little Present to receive,   10
And me, your duteous Son beleive,
                              James Edward Austen

Dirt & Slime

Here the fourteen-year-old schoolboy affectionately sends up his
father's proto-Romantic Nature poetry; in later life he lovingly made
careful transcriptions of it.

Well I remember once, Papa
When going home to see Mama
        From Kintbury so gay —
Some very pretty verses made
On every tree & hill & glade   5
        He saw upon his way.

Through these, the Muses charmed he led;
Who, pleased as Punch, well crowned his head
        With never fading Bays.
But tho' this selfsame way I rode,   10
And to the very same abode,
        Far different are my lays —

For much he praised each noble tree
Each hillock, valley, down & lea
        And all such daisyish stuff —   15
But the tenacious dirt & slime
Which keeps impressions such a time!
        I ne'er can praise enough. —

But for that charming dirt & slime
I might have wandered to some Clime   20
        Far distant, all alone.
I might have ridden into Spain

59

And ne'er have seen you all again;
Or to cold Russia gone.

I might have gone to Afric's sands,   25
Or fallen into Arab's hands
        Or on Siberia laid:
Have wandered on the banks of Tweed,
Or in the Highlands, or indeed
        Where might I not have strayed!   30

For, courteous Reader, you must know
Eer in my tale I further go
        That the preceding night;
A man & horse had gone that way
Whose footsteps deep marked in the clay   35
        Were still exposed to sight —

Thus when a good & steady hound
In the deep wood his game has found
        The best of all the pack,
Depending on his tender nose,   40
Tracing it's footsteps swift he goes
        Yet close upon it's track.

Thus, I did also, all the time
Depending on the dirt & slime
        And thus I found my way.   45
For had this road been made of stone
Or filled with gravelly soil alone
        I might have stayed all day —

And thus, in my poor humble Rhyme
The usefulness of dirt & slime   50
I'll make all people feel —
For it conducted me safe home,
No longer suffered me to roam,
        Although I ran the heel —
            Js. Ed^{wd} Austen — 1813

To Miss J. Austen

Following the publication of *Pride and Prejudice* in January 1813 the
identity of the author of this and the earlier *Sense and Sensibility* (both
published anonymously) gradually became known, largely as a
result of Henry Austen's pride in his sister's work.

No words can express, my dear Aunt, my surprise
Or make you conceive how I opened my eyes,
Like a pig Butcher Pile has just struck with his knife,
When I heard for the very first time in my life
That I had the honour to have a relation   5
Whose works were dispersed through the whole of the nation.
I assure you, however, I'm terribly glad;
Oh dear! just to think (and the thought drives me mad)
That dear Mrs Jennings's good-natured strain
Was really the produce of your witty brain,   10
That you made the Middletons, Dashwoods, and all,
And that you (not young Ferrars) found out that a ball
May be given in cottages, never so small.
And that though Mr. Collins, so grateful for all,
Will Lady de Bourgh his dear Patroness call,   15
'Tis to your ingenuity really he owed
His living, his wife, and his humble abode.
Now if you will take your poor nephew's advice,
Your works to Sir William pray send in a trice,
If he'll undertake to some grandees to show it,   20
By whose means at last the Prince Regent might know it,
For I'm sure if he did, in reward for your tale,
He'd make you a countess at least, without fail,
And indeed if the Princess should lose her dear life
You might have a good chance of becoming his wife.   25

61

CAROLINE MARY CRAVEN AUSTEN

Noun Verse

For the method of writing noun verses see the explanatory note, p.105.

Question: *Which is the prettiest brooch in the room?*
Noun: *Temper.*

(*In the Character of Mrs. Norris, Mansfield Park.*)

'If I must speak — though really I'm quite ashamed to say it —
But I think it not becoming to see her thus display it!
Her kind and generous cousins, ma'am, — her uncle — and her
                                                              aunt —
It's much handsomer than mine, or than that of Mrs. Grant!
And just this very evening too — I'd be sorry to speak loud;   5
But her poor dear mother's temper was always rather proud.'
                                                        C.M.C.

BIBLIOGRAPHY

The novels of Jane Austen: *Sense and Sensibility* (1811), *Pride and Prejudice* (1813), *Mansfield Park* (1814), *Emma* (1816), *Northanger Abbey* and *Persuasion* (1818). All references are to The Oxford Illustrated Jane Austen, ed. R.W. Chapman, Oxford, 1923. The Juvenilia and other minor works were first collected in vol. VI of the Oxford edition as *Minor Works*, ed. Chapman, 1954, rev. B.C. Southam, 1969.

References to the Letters of Jane Austen are as follows:

Brabourne *Letters*	Edward, 1st Lord Brabourne, *Letters of Jane Austen*, London, 1884.
Chapman *Letters*	R.W. Chapman, *Jane Austen's Letters to her Sister Cassandra and Others*, Oxford, 1932.
Letters	Deirdre Le Faye, *Jane Austen's Letters*, Oxford, 1995.

Abbreviations used in the text:
Unpublished

Austen-Leigh MS	MS material deriving from James Edward Austen-Leigh and his descendants; Hampshire Record Office, Winchester.
Bellas MS	8vo volume compiled 1872 by Louisa Langlois Bellas, daughter of Anna Lefroy; private collection.
Bodmer MS	Folded 4to sheet in hand of Jane Austen; Fondation Martin Bodmer, Cologny-Geneve (facs. in British Library).
Chawton MS	4to volume in hand of James Edward Austen-Leigh (*c*.1834), containing verses by James Austen; Jane Austen Memorial Trust, Chawton.
Gilson MS	Small album in unidentified hand, *c*.1830, containing 44 riddles and charades by members of the Austen family; David Gilson Esq.

Lefroy MS   4to volume in hand of Anna Lefroy (*c.*1855-
                          72); descendants of Adml. Sir Francis
                          Austen.

Published .
Charades &c.   *Charades &c. written a hundred years ago by
                          Jane Austen and her family* [Mary Augusta
                          Austen-Leigh?], London, 1895.
Critical Bibliography   R.W. Chapman, *Jane Austen – A Critical
                          Bibliography*, Oxford, 1953.
Fam. Rec.   W. & R.A. Austen-Leigh, rev. Deirdre Le
                          Faye, *Jane Austen – A Family Record*, Lon-
                          don, 1989.
Gilson   David Gilson, 'Jane Austen's Verses', *Book
                          Collector*, vol.33, no.1, Spring 1984, pp.25-
                          37; vol.34, no.3, Autumn 1985, pp.384-5.
Goodly Heritage   G.H. Tucker, *A Goodly Heritage – A history
                          of Jane Austen's family*, Manchester, 1983.
Honan   Park Honan, *Jane Austen – Her Life*, London,
                          1987.
Jane Austen and   Emma Austen-Leigh, *Jane Austen and Bath*,
Bath   London, 1939.
Jane Austen and   Emma Austen-Leigh, *Jane Austen and
Steventon*   Steventon*, London, 1937.
Letters in Facsimile   Jo Modert, *Jane Austen's Manuscript Letters
                          in Facsimile*, Carbondale and Edwardsville,
                          Ill., 1990.
Memoir   James Edward Austen-Leigh, *A Memoir of
                          Jane Austen*, London, 1870.
My Aunt Jane   Caroline Mary Craven Austen, *My Aunt
Austen*   Jane Austen*, Jane Austen Society, 1952.
Reminiscences   Caroline Mary Craven Austen, ed. Le Faye,
                          Reminiscences of Caroline Austen, Jane Austen
                          Society, 1986.

TEXTUAL NOTES

Jane Austen

1 POEMS FROM THE JUVENILIA   1787–*c*.1793. Songs and Epitaphs from *Frederic and Elfrida*, Song from *Henry and Eliza*, Ode to Pity (*Volume the First*). Source: autograph MS in the Bodleian Library, Oxford. First publ. ed. Chapman, Oxford, 1933. 2 Songs from *The First Act of a Comedy* (*Volume the Second*). Source: autograph MS in the British Library. First publ. ed. Southam, Oxford, 1963.

3 THIS LITTLE BAG   1792. Source: autograph MS in the possession of Mrs Joan Mason Hurley (Joan Austen-Leigh), reproduced in *Country Life*, 172, p.1323 (28 October 1982). First publ. *Memoir*.

4 LINES WRITTEN BY JANE AUSTEN FOR THE AMUSEMENT OF A NIECE   1806. Source: Lefroy MS. First publ. Le Faye, *TLS*, 20 Feb. 1987, p.185.

5 OH! MR BEST, YOU'RE VERY BAD   1806. Source: autograph MS in the possession of Mrs Joan Mason Hurley (Joan Austen-Leigh), transcribed by Donald Greene in 'New Verses by Jane Austen', *Nineteenth Century Fiction*, 30, 1975. pp.257-60. First publ. W. and R.A. Austen-Leigh, *Jane Austen, her Life and Letters: A Family Record*, 1913, p.70 (first 3 verses); Greene, *op. cit.* (complete). On verso: To Martha.
37   Decide [?] to go to Harrowgate *cancelled*.
42   Oh! wicked Mr Best *cancelled*.

7 ON SIR HOME POPHAM'S SENTENCE   1807. Source: facsimile of Bodmer MS. First publ. Brabourne *Letters*.

7 TO MISS BIGG PREVIOUS TO HER MARRIAGE   1808. Source: facsimile of Bodmer MS. The autograph MS originally sent (of the first of the two verses only) is now in the possession of the Jane Austen Memorial Trust at Chawton and offers a variant text. First publ. Brabourne *Letters*. Brabourne prints both *On Sir Home Popham's Sentence* and the *Verses to rhyme with 'Rose'* (see below), also from the Bodmer MS, as having been 'enclosed in one of the Letters of 1807'. Although he does not state this specifically about the *Cambrick* verses, the fact that he prints both of them, and the first bears the title given in the Bodmer MS, suggests that it was from that autograph sheet that he took them. Since the MS actually sent is dated 1808, the Bodmer MS cannot date from as early as 1807.

Variants in Chawton MS:
No title, but on verso: Miss Bigg
2   employ;] employ:
3   friend] Friend
4   Tears to wipe] tears to wipe   joy!] joy! —
    Signature: JA. — Aug;ˢᵗ 26. — 1808 —

8 TO THE MEMORY OF Mᴿˢ LEFROY   1808. Source: autograph MS in the possession of the Dean and Chapter of Winchester Cathedral (Winchester Cathedral MS XXb), to whom it was given in 1936 by Mrs Lefroy's great-grand-daughter, Jessie Lefroy. This is the fair copy of another autograph MS, the whereabouts of which are at present unknown, but two stanzas of which were transcribed in the catalogue of Sotheby's sale on 3 May 1948 (see variants below); Gilson also lists two further MSS in different hands based on the Winchester text. First publ. General Sir John Henry Lefroy, *Notes and documents relating to the family of Loffroy*, Woolwich, 1868.
Variants in the two printed verses of the earlier MS:
13   by Hamilton t'was said] 'by Burke t'was finely' *cancelled and replaced by* 'by Hamilton t'was' [Hamilton is not identified as the source of the quotation in the 1792 edn. of Boswell's *Life of Samuel Johnson, LL.D.*]
20   may] shall

10 ALAS! POOR BRAG   1809. Source: MS in the Pierpont Morgan Library, New York, reproduced in *Letters in Facsimile*. First publ. Brabourne *Letters*.

10 MY DEAREST FRANK   1809. Source: MS in the possession of the Jane Austen Memorial Trust, Chawton; this is the fair copy of the letter actually sent, which is in the British Library (Add.MS 42180; see variants below). First publ. Chapman *Letters*.
Variants in British Library MS:
    Copy of a letter to Frank, July 26. 1809.] Chawton, July 26. — 1809. —
2   boy] Boy
3   pain,] pain
4   Mary Jane.] Mary Jane. —
6   Parents Love!] Parents' Love! —
8   name] Name   Blood;] Blood,
12   spirit; —] spirit, —
17   (His...descried)] His...descried,
18   With,] With   bide'.] bide'. —

66

19 Fearless] *indented*.
22 controul] Controul
24 Bray! —] Bray.
25 Child] Child,
26 mild.] mild!
28 days] days,
29 Manhood] Manhood,   mind,] mind
30 him] him,
33 Then] *indented*.
35 Feel] Feels [*sic*]
36 know. —] know.
38 worth. —] Worth.
39 As] *indented*.   well,] well;
40 tell.] tell. —
41 give] paint   state] state,
43 home —] home,
44 it] it,   mind,] mind;
45 convinced] convinced,   complete,] complete
49 You'll] *no indent*.   year;] year,
50 near —] near,
52 us.] us. —
J.A.] J.A. —

12 IN MEASURED VERSE 1810? Source: *Memoir* (no known MS).

13 I'VE A PAIN IN MY HEAD 1811. Source: reproduction in sale catalogue of autograph MS sold at Christies 16 Dec. 1991 (lot 275, p.141); the MS, which descended through Anna Lefroy, has on verso part of Mrs Austen's Riddle on the letter O, wrongly assumed in all catalogues to be by Cassandra Elizabeth Austen (see p.37). A second autograph MS is in the Winchester City Museum; it is on a leaf torn from a notebook and is probably the earlier of the two. A third MS, in the hand of Anna Lefroy (Lefroy MS), has the same speech marks as the first MS above, while the Winchester MS has none; it seems likely therefore that they were added to JA's MS by Anna Lefroy (I have nevertheless printed them). First publ. *MW*. Textual variants in Winchester MS:

No speech marks; 2nd and 4th lines in each verse indented.
2 Beckford] Beckford,
3 dread] dread.
4 Ah!] Oh!   for't.] for't? [But question mark probably added by Anna Lefroy.]

5   her] this
7   head,] head
9   Beckford] Beckford,
12 Calomel] calomel   brisk.] brisk. —
13 praise-worthy] praiseworthy   notion!] notion.
14 Newnham] Newnham,
Jane Austen] *No signature, but the date*: Feby. 1811. —
    *At a right-angle to the date and the last three lines of the poem is another
    date*: Jany. 1810 —, *referring to something on a part of the paper now
    removed.*

14 ON THE MARRIAGE OF MR GELL OF EAST BOURN TO MISS GILL 1811. Source:
autograph MS in the possession of Park Honan reproduced in Sotheby's
sale catalogue of 14 March 1979 (Lor 296). Another autograph MS is
owned by Bath City Council and has *When stretch'd on one's bed* on the
same sheet. First publ. *Memoir* in a version which differs from both the
above MSS; since they descended through the family of Charles Austen,
a third MS not now known is likely to have been owned by the Austen-
Leighs.
Variants in the Bath MS:
    Title: On reading in the Newspaper, the Marriage of 'Mr Gell of
    Eastbourne to Miss Gill.' —
    No indentations.
1   Eastbourn,] Eastbourne
4   Love] love
6   I'm] 'I'm   i.s] *eyes.*
7   Ah!] Oh!
8   e.s. —] *ease.'*
    Signature: J.A.   *On fourth side*: For Captn Austen R.N.

15 BETWEEN SESSION & SESSION 1811. Source: autograph MS in the Pier-
pont Morgan Library, New York, reproduced in *Letters in Facsimile*. First
publ. Brabourne *Letters*.

15 WHEN STRETCH'D ON ONE'S BED 1811. Source: autograph MS in the
possession of Bath City Council (see *On the marriage of Mr Gell*, above).
There is a copy in the Lefroy MS, headed (wrongly): Lines written at
Winchester by Jane Austen during her last illness. — First publ. *MW*.
10-12 How little one thinks[?]
         Of the Smells[?] or the Stinks[?]
       Which pervade the Assembly all[?] *cancelled*; 10-12 *added superscript*.
21 attract] *added superscript*;   catch *cancelled*.

v.5   For our bodily[?] pains
         Ev'ry faculty chains.
    We can feel on no subject beside.
     'Tis for Health & for Ease
     The F[*illeg.*] powers to seize
    For their[?] Friends[?] &[?] their Souls to provide.
cancelled. V.5 as printed added below.

16 ON THE MARRIAGE OF MISS CAMILLA WALLOP   1812. Source: Lefroy MS. First publ. *Memoir*, where 'Maria' is substituted for 'Camilla', and instead of being 'merry, & small' is described as 'handsome, and tall'. Stephen Terry, of Dummer, noted the verse in his diary, 13 April 1860:

> Camilla good humoured & merry & small
> For a Husband it happend was at her last stake;
> & having in vain danced at many a ball
> Is now very happy to Jump at a Wake.

These lines given to me this day by Mrs Ben Lefroy here, Georgies Mother; they were written by her very clever Relation Miss Jane Austen, the celebrated Novelist, about the beginning [of] the Century. (Quoted in *Letters*, p.409.)

Gilson suggests that this is what JA refers to as the 'Steventon Edition' (i.e. the version amended by James Austen); but that is more likely to be the *Memoir* version, in which J.E. Austen-Leigh maintained the disguise that had presumably been suggested by his father. Anna Lefroy would no doubt have given Stephen Terry the version she copied into her album, and he may well have noted it down wrongly. The verse predates the marriage by at least four months – the title is as given in the Lefroy MS; Anna Lefroy was unaware of the reference in the letter of 1812 (which was in the possession of Francis Austen's family): Chapman, who did know it (see no.74.1 of his edition of the *Letters*), has less excuse for using the word 'marriage' in *MW*, where he repeats the title from the version printed in the *Memoir*. Anna Lefroy leaves a space for Mr Wake's Christian name.

17 WRITTEN AT WINCHESTER   1817. Source: MS in the possession of the Jane Austen Memorial Trust at Chawton, in a hand similar to JA's 'but probably not hers' (Gilson); it descended through the family of Charles Austen. A second MS, in an unidentified hand (Honan suggests Mary Lloyd, but there is little resemblance) is in the Berg Collection of the New York Public Library; the alterations suggest that it may have been dictated

by JA. There is also a copy in the Lefroy MS. First publ. J.H. and E.C. Hubback, *Jane Austen's sailor brothers*, London, 1906; for Caroline Austen's reasons for not wishing to comply with Lord Stanhope's request to make the verses, mentioned in the *Memoir*, public ('the joke about the dead Saint, & the Winchester races, all jumbled up together, would read badly as amongst the few details given, of the closing scene...'), see Le Faye, 'Jane Austen's Verses and Lord Stanhope's Disappointment', *Book Collector*, 37:1, Spring 1988, pp.86-91. The title *Venta* was given by Chapman in *MW*.
Variants in New York MS:

    Title] No title is given.

  1 their] thier

  3 S^t:] Saint

  4 Wykham's] Wykehams

  5 fix'd] fixed   determin'd] determined

  6 met &] came and

  7 &] and   sattin'd & ermin'd] satined & ermined

  8 alarming.] alarming. —

10 roof] Roof

12 address'd] addressed

13 rebellious,] rebellious!   Venta] Venta[r *cancelled*]

14 dead] gone

15 Immortal. —] immortal!   you're] you'r

14-15 When...immortal! *underlined*.

16 You have] Youe *cancelled*; You've have [*sic*]   sinn'd] sinned
     suffer. —] suffer,   further] farther   he said *superscript*.
     [*This line comes over the page, which may account for the non-rhyme.*]

17 &...&] and...and

19 you shall] You s[h *added superscript*]   all   pleasures] *superscript*.

20 your course] your [curse *cancelled*] course   my] *my*

21 July.] July

22 powers,] powers

24 Venta] Ventar   showers.] showers —
     No signature.

18 RIDDLES n.d. Source: Gilson MS. Nos.2 and 3 also in Lefroy MS. First publ. *Charades &c.*
Variants in Lefroy MS:
No.2

 2 and Powers] & Powers;

 3 Man] Man,   [*For* a Man who oft *Charades &c. prints* a monster, who.]

No signature.

No.3
1   stream] stream,
2   second] 2^d   adore] adore;
3   if] if,   whole] whole,
4   diminish,] diminish —
    Jane] Jane Austen

19 CHARADE *c.*1814. Source: *Emma*, vol.1, ch.9. First publ. 1816.

Family Verse

20 LINES *SUPPOSED* TO HAVE BEEN SENT TO AN UNCIVIL DRESSMAKER and MISS
GREEN'S REPLY   1805. Source: Lefroy MS. First publ. Le Faye, *TLS*, 20 Feb.
1987, p.185. Titles probably supplied by Anna Lefroy.

21 VERSES TO RHYME WITH 'ROSE'   1807. Source: facsimile of Bodmer MS.
The verses by JA and Cassandra also exist, with variants, in MSS by
Fanny Lefroy (daughter of Anna), Hampshire Record Office, 23M93/85/
1/1,2. First publ. Brabourne *Letters*.

23 BOUTS-RIMÉS   1820. Source: [R.A. Austen-Leigh,] *Bouts-Rimés and
Noun Verses*, Eton, *c.*1905[?] (no known MS).

Mrs Austen

25 EPISTLE TO G. EAST ESQ^R   1779. Source: MS in Anna Lefroy's hand,
Hampshire Record Office, 23M93/58/1. Two copies in Lefroy MS, one (A)
by Anna Lefroy, the other (B) possibly in a different hand.
Significant variants in Lefroy MS:
11   creates] invents (B)
21   The story] And the story
24   there are] there's
26   you have stay'd] you ve delayed (B)
42   lie by] go by
51   is here] we have
    Added below (A): I am obliged for these playful lines (written by my
    Grandmother to an absent Pupil of her Husband's) to the Revd J.B.
    Harrison Rector of Evenley Brackley — Northamptonshire
    Signature (B): C. Austen.

27 TO F.S. *c.*1780. Source: MS in Anna Lefroy's hand, Hampshire Record Office, 23M93/58/1. Copy in Lefroy MS following, and in the hand of, (B) above. The first 4 verses quoted in *Honan*.
Significant variants in Lefroy MS:

> *Title*] To F Stewart who accused the writer of partiality in writing verses to F C Fowle & not to him.

15   look] grow
24   who] that
34   ere] eer
> *Signature*: C Austen

28 THE HUMBLE PETITION   *c.*1791. Source: MS in the hand of R.A. Austen-Leigh, Hampshire Record Office, 23M93/97/4. First publ. *Jane Austen and Steventon*.

29 I SEND YOU HERE   dated 1794, but probably later (see explanatory note). Source: Lefroy MS. Another MS in Anna Lefroy's hand, Hampshire Record Office, 23M93/58/1. First publ. *Jane Austen and Bath*.
Significant variants in Hampshire MS:

7   his] *his*
> Sent...home] C. Austen — 1794 —

30 DIALOGUE BETWEEN DEATH AND M^{RS} A: 1804. Source: autograph MS, Hampshire Record Office, 23M93/103/3. First publ. *Jane Austen and Bath*.

31 FABLES   n.d. Source: autograph MS as *Dialogue* above.

32 A RECEIPT FOR A PUDDING   1808? Source: MS in the hand of Martha Lloyd ('Martha Lloyd's Household Book'), ff.7-9, in the possession of the Jane Austen Memorial Trust, Chawton. First publ. *Goodly Heritage*.

34 I HOPE, MY ANNA   1814. Source: facsimile of autograph MS in the Robert Taylor Collection, Princeton University Library. Copies in Lefroy MS, Hampshire Record Office, 23M93/58/1/4 and Bellas MS.

36 RIDDLES AND CHARADES NOS.1-5   n.d. Sources: no.1: autograph MS in Hampshire Record Office, 23M93/103/3 (also containing *Dialogue between Death and M^{rs} A*: and Fables, above); nos.2-5: transcription by Deirdre Le Faye of autograph MS in the possession of the descendants of Adml. Charles Austen, consecutive with the preceding (both sheets have the same watermark of 1797): they are a collection of fair copies made some time after 1804. Nos.3 and 4 also in Lefroy MS, signed respectively 'C. Austen l'ainée' and 'Cassandra Austen ainée'. No.4 (ll.3-14) also on verso of *Maria Beckford* MS (see above p.67) and quoted in part in *Honan* and more fully in *Gilson*, pp.384-5, in both cases wrongly attributed to Cassandra Elizabeth Austen.

38 RIDDLES AND CHARADES NOS. 6-9   n.d. Source: Gilson MS. Nos.6-8 first publ. *Charades &c.*

James Austen

With the exception of the *Lines in memory of his sister*, no autograph MS is known of any of the poems printed here, which are found in two collections copied by his son James Edward Austen-Leigh some time after 1834 (the date of the watermarks). The first of these, in the possession of the Jane Austen Memorial Trust at Chawton, contains 40 poems and 14 enigmas; the second, in the Austen-Leigh archive, Hampshire Record Office 23M93/60/3/2, contains 23 of the Chawton poems and 4 others, including James Austen's most ambitious work, *The Recovery of Rural Life*, which extended to 849 lines and was left unfinished at his death. There are 6 poems in an unidentified hand in the Hampshire Record Office (23M93/60/3/1), two of them not in either of James Edward Austen-Leigh's collections.

40 EPILOGUE TO THE SULTAN   1790. Source: Chawton MS. Significant variants in Austen-Leigh MS:
     5   that] the
    13   tried] tied
    48   Vizier] Viziers   Aga] Agas

42 TO EDWARD ON THE DEATH OF HIS FIRST PONY   1811. Source: Chawton MS. Significant variants in Austen-Leigh MS:
        Jany 30th 1811 *added after title*.
     8-9 *Lines reversed*.
    40   boy] son
    50   kindly] lively
    54   in] on
    60   tried] wearied
    63   or] &
    84   soon] sure
    99   in] on
   106   such] each
        No date.

45 TYGER'S LETTER TO CAROLINE   1812. Source: Chawton MS. First publ. *Goodly Heritage*.

46 ADDRESS TO TYGER   1812. Source: Chawton MS. Significant variants in Austen-Leigh MS:
18   Since] If
41   ever] any
49   Midst] 'Mongst
50   lesson] terror

48 VENTA! WITHIN THY SACRED FANE   1817. Source: autograph MS in the possession of the Warden and Fellows' Library, Winchester College, where there is also a second MS, possibly in the hand of Henry Austen. There is a copy by James Edward Austen-Leigh in the Austen-Leigh MS. First publ. *Goodly Heritage*. Significant variants in the Henry Austen (HA) and Austen-Leigh (A-L) MSS:

    Title: *Lines* To the memory of his sister, Jane Austen, who died at Winchester, July 18th 1817, & was buried in that Cathedral. (A-L) By the Revd J. Austen (HA *in pencil*)
11   his] this (HA, A-L)
13   Chapels] Chapel (HA, A-L)
32   descry] espy (HA, A-L)
33   ever *omitted in A-L.*
48   displaced] misplaced (HA, A-L)
72   Angles] Angels (HA, A-L)
74   attendant] Eternal (HA) eternal (A-L)
    dated below: 1817 (HA)

50 TO MISS JANE AUSTEN   1811[?]. Source: autograph[?] MS in the possession of David Gilson. The MS is in a disguised hand and was attributed by Chapman, who first published it in the *Critical Bibliography*, to James Edward Austen-Leigh; Deirdre Le Faye points out, however, that James Edward was only thirteen at the time *S&S* was published, and the tone is not that of a young boy to his aunt; furthermore his own poem expressing surprise at the discovery that JA was an author (p.61) was not written until after the appearance of *P&P* in 1813. The Alton postmark seems to confirm James Austen's authorship.

51 CHARADE, n.d. Source: Gilson MS. First publ. *Charades &c*.

James Leigh Perrot

52 ON CAPT. FOOTE'S MARRIAGE WITH MISS PATTON   1803. Source: MS in the hand of Jane Austen[?] in the Pierpont Morgan Library, New York, MA1034, transcribed in *Jane Austen Letters & Manuscripts in the Pierpont Morgan Library*, New York, 1975. First publ. *Memoir*.

52 RIDDLES   n.d. Source: Gilson MS. Also included in large collection of unattributed riddles, charades, logogriphs and rebuses made *c*.1800[?] by Eliza Chute, of The Vyne, near Basingstoke, Hampshire Record Office, 23M93/70/4. Nos.1 and 2 first publ. *Charades &c*. Significant variants in Chute MS:
1. This occurs twice in Chute MS, with variants only in first version, which is laid out in 4 verses of 4 lines each, the 2nd and 4th lines indented.
1   both] we
3   nor heads nor mouths] nor head nor mouth
6   We are from passion always free] From passion we are always free
3. *In 4-line verses, 2nd and 4th lines indented*.

Cassandra Elizabeth Austen
54 CHARADES   n.d. Source: Gilson MS. First publ. *Charades &c*.

Francis William Austen
54 CHARADE   n.d. Source: Gilson MS. First publ. *Charades &c*.

Charles John Austen
55 CHARADE   n.d. Source: Gilson MS. First publ. *Charades &c*. wrongly attributed to Revd George Austen.

Henry Thomas Austen

55 CHARADE   n.d. Source: Gilson MS. First publ. *Charades &c.*, in which, presumably for reasons of propriety, the Housemaid has become a 'Foot-boy' and the ill natured Jade an 'unruly rogue'.

56 GODMERSHAM THE TEMPLE OF DELIGHT   n.d. Source: Lefroy MS.

George Knight
56 GEORGE KNIGHT TO HIS DOG PINCHER   n.d. Source: Lefroy MS.

Jane Anna Elizabeth Austen (Anna Lefroy)
57 ON READING A LETTER   1809. Source: MS in the hand of Fanny Knight, Kent Archives Office, U.951.C211. First publ. Margaret Wilson, 'Anna Austen's poems and her attachment to Mr Terry', Jane Austen Society *Report* for 1987.

Fanny Knight
57 TO ANNA ELIZA AUSTEN   1809. Source: autograph MS on first page of Diary for 1810, Hampshire Record Office, 39M89/F24/7. A fair copy is in Kent Archives Office MS U.951.C211. 3rd verse quoted in Maragaret Wilson, *Almost another sister*, Kent, 1990. Significant variants in Kent MS:
   To Anna Eliza Austen] To Miss J.A.E. Austen
9   introspection] retrospection

James Edward Austen-Leigh

58 LINES ADDRESSED TO HIS FATHER   n.d. Source: autograph MS, Hampshire Record Office, 23M93/60/2/5. A copy in the hand of Cholmeley Austen-Leigh, Hampshire Record Office, 23M93/86/5/1.

59 DIRT & SLIME   1813. Source: MS in hand of Cholmeley Austen-Leigh, Hampshire Record Office, 23M93/86/5/1.

61 TO MISS J. AUSTEN   1813[?]. Source: Mary Augusta Austen-Leigh, *Personal Aspects of Jane Austen*, London, 1920 (no known MS). First publ. Mary Augusta Austen-Leigh, *James Edward Austen-Leigh, a memoir by his daughter*, privately printed, 1911.

Caroline Mary Craven Austen
62 NOUN VERSE   n.d. Source: [R.A. Austen-Leigh,] *Bouts-Rimés and Noun Verses*, Eton, *c*.1905[?] (no known MS).

EXPLANATORY NOTES

Jane Austen

1 SONG (*Frederic & Elfrida*, ch.1). The cousins Elfrida and Frederic Falknor take a walk in a 'Grove of Poplars' with Elfrida's 'intimate freind' Charlotte, whose father is the Rector of Crankhumdunberry. 'In this Grove they had scarcely remained above 9 hours, when they were suddenly agreably surprized by hearing a most delightfull voice warble the following stanza.'

1 *Damon* Like 'Corydon', 'Strephon' and 'Chloe', the name is drawn from the language of pastoral poetry.

1 EPITAPH (*Frederic & Elfrida*, ch.4). 'Not being able to make any one miserable', the unfortunate Charlotte finds herself engaged to two gentlemen simultaneously, whereupon 'the reflection of her past folly, operated so strongly on her mind, that she resolved to be guilty of a greater, & to that end threw herself into a deep stream which ran thro' her Aunt's pleasure Grounds in Portland Place. She floated to Crankhumdunberry where she was picked up & buried; the following epitaph, composed by Frederic Elfrida & Rebecca [a friend], was placed on her tomb.... These sweet lines, as pathetic as beautifull were never read by any one who passed that way, without a shower of tears, which if they should fail of exciting in you, Reader, your mind must be unworthy to peruse them.'

4 *Portland Place* JA was taken to London, probably for the first time, in July 1788; the width and grandeur of Portland Place, which had been built ten years before, clearly impressed her enough to suggest the joke of pleasure grounds and water running through it.

1 SONG (*Frederic & Elfrida*, ch.4).

4 *fess.* 'To be *fess* is to be set up, elated, in high spirits.' (*A Glossary of Hampshire Words and Phrases*, ed. Revd Sir William Cope, Bart., London 1883.)

2 SONG (*Henry and Eliza*). Eliza Harcourt, brought up by her adoptive parents to have 'a Love of Virtue & a Hatred of Vice', so that she was 'the delight of all who knew her', happens one day 'to be detected in stealing a banknote of 50£'; 'turned out of doors by her inhuman Benefactors', she amuses herself, 'happy in the conscious knowledge of her own Excellence ... with making & singing the following Lines' ...

2 2 SONGS   (*The first Act of a Comedy*).

3 ODE TO PITY.   The less than straightfaced dedication prepares us for the burlesque of the eighteenth-century descriptive ode that follows. Both William Collins and Joseph Warton had written Odes to Pity and, though Warton's was unpublished, JA would have known Collins's from Dodsley's *Collection* (see Introduction). Collins and Warton were both scholars at Winchester, Warton eventually becoming headmaster there in 1756. The picturesque melancholy of their imagery is turned upside-down here, where 'silent' streams brawl 'noisy' down turnpike roads, and abbeys, 'conceal'd by aged pines', rear their heads to 'take a peep'. The final joke is of course that, for all its language of generalised sympathy, the poem never alludes to pity at all.

   2   *the Myrtle Grove* Cf. Collins's 'Ode to Pity':

> There first the Wren thy Myrtles shed
> On gentlest *Otway*'s infant Head,
>   To Him thy Cell was shown;
> And while He sung the Female Heart,
> With Youth's soft Notes unspoil'd by Art,
>   Thy Turtles mix'd their own.

   (*The Works of William Collins*, ed. Wendorf and Ryskamp, OUP, 1979.)

   5   *Philomel* The nightingale.

   8   *brawling* 'Flowing with noise and commotion, as a brook' (OED).

  12 *Lovely Scenes* The phrase is ironic: the images that follow are of the kind of fashionable gothic horror literature beloved of Catherine Morland in *NA*.

  13 *Cot* 'A little cottage...connoting smallness and humbleness, rather than the meanness and rudeness expressed by *hut*' (OED).

  13 *Grot* Grotto.

  14 *the Abbey too a mouldering heap* Cf. Joseph Warton, 'Ode to Fancy', also in Dodsley:

> Let us with silent footsteps go
> To charnels and the house of woe;
> To Gothic churches, vaults, and tombs,
> Where each sad night some virgin comes
> With throbbing breast and faded cheek
> Her promised bridegroom's urn to seek.
> Or to some abbey's mouldering towers...

3 THIS LITTLE BAG.   Jane Austen's niece Caroline, daughter of the recipient, was to recall of her aunt that 'she was fond of work [i.e. needlework] — and she was a great adept at overcast and satin stitch — the peculiar delight of that day — General handiness and neatness were amongst her characteristics' (*My Aunt Jane Austen*, p.7).

5   *This little bag*   In the *Memoir*, ch.5, James Edward Austen-Leigh writes, 'In a very small bag is deposited a little rolled up housewife, furnished with minikin needles and fine thread. In the housewife is a tiny pocket, and in the pocket is enclosed a slip of paper, on which, written with a crow quill, are these lines.' His great-granddaughter, Joan Austen-Leigh, further describes the bag in an article in *Country Life* (28 Oct. 1982, p.1323) as being, like the housewife itself, 'made of white cotton with gold and black zigzag stripes'; the 'tiny pocket' containing the folded paper is concealed beneath a red flannel needle-holder.

4 LINES WRITTEN FOR THE AMUSEMENT OF A NIECE.   Supposedly spoken by the thirteen-year-old girl, the poem captures a sense of the child's voice in the breathless excitement before the visitors' arrival and in the list of places she imagines them passing through, almost as if she were tracing their journey on a map.

3   *Richard Kennet*   This may be Richard Kennett, a neighbour of Edward Knight in Wye, Kent, or his four-year-old son, also called Richard. In any case, the name is a gift to the rhyme-scheme.

4   *the Parents of the Bride*   Mr and Mrs John Gibson of Ramsgate.

10   *the Park*   Godmersham had been rebuilt and the park laid out in 1732 by the father of Thomas Knight, Edward Austen's benefactor.

13   *the Pier gate*   The main gate in the brick wall surrounding the park is embellished with tall pillars, or 'piers' (also of brick).

5 OH! MR BEST, YOU'RE VERY BAD.   On 2 July 1806 Mrs Austen and her daughters moved from Bath to Clifton, the western suburb of Bristol built above the Hotwell spa, where they remained for the rest of that month. With them was Martha Lloyd, who, since the death of her mother the previous year (see p.87), had made her home with them, and was to remain a member of the household until after Mrs Austen's death in 1827, when she eventually became the second wife of Francis Austen. In view of the ironic suggestion that he 'may not live another year', one presumes that Mr Best was not shown these verses, which in any case have the playful tone of a joke intended for an intimate family friend. Mr Best has not been identified; he may have been a resident of Clifton, or perhaps he visited the spa for his health. There must of course have been many reasons for his not taking Martha to Harrogate, supposing that such a suggestion such a suggestion was ever seriously made; it seems more likely that mention of her impending visit came up by chance and that the poem was subsequently written as a joke, inspired, characteristically, by the gentleman's name.

10   *The Posting not increased*   The distance – and therefore the inconvenience – has not grown any greater.

11   *You're scarcely stouter than you were...*   'You're hardly in better health than you were...'

19   *Richard's pills*   The Royal Pharmaceutical Society has no record of any proprietary medicine of this name; but Bristol and Bath newspapers of the time carried advertisements for 'Robberd's Improved Balsamic Elixir or Cough Drops'. JA replaced 'Robberd' with 'Richard', a name that had become a family joke (Catherine Morland's father was 'a very respectable man, though his name was Richard', *NA* ch.1, p.13); for the connection of this name with the flagship the *Bonhomme Richard* in the American War of Independence, see F.B. Pinion, '...though his name was Richard', Jane Austen Society *Report* for 1993.

36   *From Newb'ry to Speen Hill*   A distance of one mile. At Speen Hill in Berkshire lived Mrs Craven, a widowed aunt of Martha Lloyd often visited by Jane and Cassandra. The shadow of John Gilpin's runaway horse, in JA's beloved Cowper, is galloping somewhere behind these verses, though over different terrain:

> Said John, it is my wedding-day,
> And all the world would stare,
> If wife should dine at Edmonton,
> And I should dine at Ware.

37   *Morton's wife*   'If you do not return in time to send the Turkey yourself, we must trouble you for Mr Morton's direction again, as we should be quite as much at a loss as ever. It becomes now a sort of vanity in us not to know Mr Morton's direction with any certainty.' *Letter* from JA (at Chawton) to Martha Lloyd, 29 November 1812 (*Letters*, p.197).

7 ON SIR HOME POPHAM'S SENTENCE.   The trial of Sir Home Riggs Popham was held at Portsmouth on 6 March 1807, the charge being that he had withdrawn his squadron from the Cape of Good Hope, leaving Cape Town unprotected, in order to take William Carr Beresford's forces to Buenos Aires to fight the Spanish. I am grateful to Brian Southam for pointing out that Francis Austen, while serving in his first ship, the *Perseverance*, came to the notice of William Cornwallis, his Squadron Commodore in the East Indies, whose brother, the Governor General of India, was a friend of Popham; subsequently Francis organised the North Foreland unit of the Sea Fencibles in Ramsgate in 1803-4, a line of defence that Popham had founded. This family connection doubtless accounts for the unusually sharp satire of JA's verse. Popham's career was ultimately unaffected by the sentence: he was presented with a sword of honour by the City of London, appointed KCB in 1815, and was C.-in-C. of the Jamaica Station 1817-20.

1   *a Ministry*   Grenville's Ministry of All the Talents, for whose failures in the prosecution of the Napoleonic War Popham had been made something of a scapegoat, fell on 25 March 1807.

3   *stand*   The word can be read 'backwards' (he stands for these qualities) or 'forwards' (he stands condemned). The neat and forceful ambiguity of a word strongly placed at the end of the line prepares for the scathing, epigrammatic conclusion.

7   *warrant*   Authorise (possibly also 'deserve').

7 TO MISS BIGG.   The first two lines of each poem emphasise JA's enjoyment of needlework. The second version cheerily acknowledges a variety of uses for the handkerchiefs that the more staid verse actually sent does not choose to recognise.

     Miss Bigg   Catherine Bigg, of Manydown Park, was the sister of Harris Bigg-Wither, whose proposal of marriage JA had accepted on the evening of 2 December 1802, only to change her mind the next morning. In October 1808 Catherine married the Revd Herbert Hill, uncle of the poet Robert Southey.

1   *Cambrick*   A kind of fine white linen, originally made at Cambray in Flanders [OED].

6   *To bear her name*   Possibly JA had embroidered Miss Bigg's name on the handkerchiefs.

8 TO THE MEMORY OF M^RS^ LEFROY.   The poem was written on or about the fourth anniversary of Mrs Lefroy's death.

13   *At Johnson's death...*   In the *Life* Boswell quotes Johnson's friend the Rt. Hon. William Gerrard Hamilton (1727?-96): 'Johnson is dead. — Let us go to the next best. — There is nobody. — No man can be said to put you in mind of Johnson.' (1792 edn, vol.3, pp.563-4.) For JA's earlier misattribution of the remark to Burke see textual note.

22   *to thee*   I.e. 'compared to thee'.

27   *Countenance almost divine*   The phraseology no doubt derives from stock eighteenth-century religious writing; the similarity to 'And did the Countenance Divine/Shine forth upon our clouded hills?' (from

Blake's preface to *Milton*, engraved 1804-9) is presumably coincidental.

42   *Her partial favour*   The 'smiles benign' of l.25 are here intensified into an expression of particular love for the author, but at the same moment 'the Vision disappears' (recalling perhaps Milton's sonnet 'On his Deceased Wife').

10 'ALAS! POOR BRAG'.   In a letter of of 10 January 1809, JA writes to Cassandra at Godmersham on the subject of card games currently popular with the Kent family, having presumably been told in an earlier letter that their nephew Edward had been playing more brag than speculation: 'The preference of Brag over Speculation does not greatly surprise me I beleive, because I feel the same myself; but it mortifies me deeply, because Speculation was under my patronage' (*Letters*, pp.163-4). In another letter to Cassandra, dated Tuesday 17 January 1809, she includes the verse, which she pretends was delivered anonymously: 'I have just received some verses in an unknown hand, & am desired to forward them to my nephew Edwd at Godmersham. —' (*Letters*, p.167.) The opening apostrophe, 'Alas! poor Brag', as well as the subsequent questions, recall *Hamlet*. A week later she writes: 'I am sorry my verses did not bring any return from Edward, I was in hopes they might — but I suppose he does not rate them high enough. — It might be partiality, but they seemed to me purely classical — just like Homer & Virgil, Ovid & Propria que Maribus [a lesson in the Eton Latin Grammar].' (*Letters*, p.170.)

      Brag   Similar to poker. 'The name is taken from the "brag" or challenge given by one of the players to the rest to turn up cards equal in value to his.' (OED) It affords an apt pun.

   5   *Speculation*   'A round game of cards, the chief feature of which is the buying and selling of trump cards, the player who possesses the highest trump in a round winning the pool.' (OED) It is the game Henry Crawford teaches Fanny and Lady Bertram to play (see *M.P.* vol.II, ch.7, p.240).

10 MY DEAREST FRANK.   After a brief congratulatory opening, the main theme of the poem is not so much the baby as a loving reminiscence of Francis William's own characteristics as a child and a wish to see them extended into the new generation.

   4   *Mary Jane*   The birth of their first child on 27 April 1807 had been a difficult one.

   18   *Bet*   The nurserymaid.

   18   *my be not come to bide*   I won't stay long!

   43   *Our Chawton home*   Mrs Austen and her daughters had moved to Chawton Cottage on 7 July.

52   *over-right us*   Edward lent the Great House at Chawton to both Francis and Charles for their shore leaves; Charles and his wife did not, however, return to England from the West Indies, until the summer of 1811.

12 IN MEASURED VERSE.   Despite James Edward Austen-Leigh's comment that 'all this nonsense is nearly extempore, and...the fancy of drawing the images from America arose at the moment from the obvious rhyme which presented itself in the first stanza', the poem is far from being nonsense. Though the absence of any MS makes certain dating impossible, it may well, as Deirdre Le Faye points out (*Fam. Rec.* 161-2), have been written during the summer of 1810, when the seventeen-year-old Anna was sent to Chawton after breaking off her engagement to the Revd Michael Terry, a match that her parents opposed, and which, her daughter Fanny Caroline wrote years later, 'would have been about as suitable as one between Lizzie Bennet & Mr. Collins'. Anna's volatile character was often a worry to her family; even when she later became engaged to the much more suitable Ben Lefroy (see p.34), JA wrote to Francis Austen, 'We are anxious to have it go on well, there being quite as much in his favour as the Chances are likely to give her in any Matrimonial connection...There is an unfortunate dissimularity of Taste between them in one respect which gives us some apprehensions, he hates company & she is very fond of it; — This, with some queerness of Temper on his side & much unsteadiness on hers, is untoward' (*Letters*, 231-2). This poem therefore may be seen as a 'mock panegyric' in more senses than one: the teasing hyperbole offers both a mild rebuke and a gentle warning to a young person whose judgment, though generally 'sound', occasionally seems sufficiently 'thick, 'black' and unfathomable to require the kind of admonitory irony that her aunt so often allows to descend in the novels 'on foes and friends'.

4   *savannah*   The OED defines the term as 'a treeless plain; properly, one of those found in various parts of tropical America'. Charles Austen served on the North American Station from 1804 to 1810 as commander of the *Indian*.

13 I'VE A PAIN IN MY HEAD.   Since calomel was generally administered as a lively purgative, presumably its principal effect on Miss Beckford was to take her mind off her headache! The joke is, of course, that the cure is suggested by the patient, whereupon the 'Doctor so dread' is so taken with the idea that he proposes to try it himself. Cf. *Elegant Extracts*, 'The Doctor and the Patient':

Slept you well? 'Very well.' My draught did good.
'It did no harm; for yonder it hath stood.'

14 ON THE MARRIAGE OF MR GELL OF EAST BOURN TO MISS GILL.   The *Hampshire Telegraph and Sussex Chronicle* of 25 February 1811 carried the announcement: 'Sussex, Saturday, February 23, 1811. On Saturday was married, Mr. Gell, of Eastbourn, to Miss Gill, of Well-street, Hackney.'

15 BETWEEN SESSION & SESSION.   Following this verse in the letter JA comments: 'There is poetry for Edward and his daughter [i.e. Fanny]'.

   Session   I.e. of Parliament.

2   *The first Prepossession*   JA probably means that in the interim the initial purchasing of land on the part of the speculators will arouse so much opposition that the Bill will be taken no further. In fact it was eventually passed, but the project failed. In the same letter another rhyme is included, clearly in reply to a request from Cassandra: 'Oh! yes, I remember Miss Emma Plumbtree's *Local* consequence perfectly. —

   "I am in a Dilemma, for want of an Emma,"

   Escaped from the Lips, Of Henry Gipps —'

Emma Maria Plumptre was the daughter of Kentish friends of Edward and his family; in 1814 her brother John Pemberton nearly became engaged to Fanny. Emma was to marry Henry (later Revd Henry) Gipps in 1812. The two lines were presumably from a game of consequences played some time previously at Godmersham; though they are assumed to be by Jane Austen, they could have been contributed by another player.

15 WHEN STRETCH'D ON ONE'S BED.   The last line gives us a jolt and invites us to adjust our reading of the poem: the 'grandest affairs' of the world have been light-heartedly evoked in terms of balls and dinners, with the odd throwaway jest such as the irreverent 'flounces or hearts'; and the bells ringing for the marrying of the bride or the carrying of the corpse seem to be nothing more than the expression of an all-inclusive range of experience. But in the last verse the headache is generalised and intensified into 'our...bodily pains', thus widening and deepening the concerns of the poem, so that the ending offers a little stricture.

8   *Waltzes and reels*   The waltz was only just entering England from the Continent and was much disapproved of. Byron's denunciation, '*The Waltz: an Apostrophic Hymn*', was published in 1812.

12   *flounce*   Ornamental strip sewn onto a dress. 'I beleive I put five breadths of Linen also into my flounce; I know I found it wanted more than I had expected, & that I sh^d have been distressed if I had not bought more than I beleived myself to need...' (*Letters*, p.123).

17   *Sauces & Stews*   Stews, or ragouts, were regarded during the

84

eighteenth century as indicative of a fashionable table; thus in *P&P* when the epicurean Mr Hurst finds that Elizabeth prefers 'a plain dish to a ragout', he has 'nothing to say to her'.

23 *Corse* Corpse.

16 ON THE MARRIAGE OF MISS CAMILLA WALLOP & THE REV^D [HENRY] WAKE. In a letter to Martha Lloyd, 29 November 1812, JA writes, 'The 4 lines on Miss W. which I sent you were all my own, but James afterwards suggested what I thought a great improvement & as it stands in the Steventon Edition' (*Letters*, pp.196-7). In the altered version from Steventon rectory James Austen substituted the name Maria, presumably so that the verse might be circulated. In this form it was printed in the *Memoir*, with the title ON THE MARRIAGE OF A MIDDLE-AGED FLIRT WITH A MR. WAKE, WHOM, IT WAS SUPPOSED, SHE WOULD SCARCELY HAVE ACCEPTED IN HER YOUTH. For the history of this verse see textual note.

1 *Camilla* Camilla Catherine Urania Wallop was born in 1774. In a letter to Cassandra, 8-11 April 1805, JA says that she has written to Charles (serving on the North American Station) 'in consequence of my Mother's having seen in the papers that the Urania was waiting at Portsmouth for the Convoy to Halifax; — this is nice, as it is only three weeks ago that you wrote by the Camilla. — The Wallop race seem very fond of Nova Scotia' (*Letters*, p.101). Scanning the shipping news for means to communicate with Charles, the Austens must have been amused by the coincidence of the names.

17 WRITTEN AT WINCHESTER. On 24 May 1817, in her last illness, JA was taken to lodgings at 8 College Street, Winchester, to be under the supervision of Mr Lyford, Surgeon-in-Ordinary at the County Hospital. Attended by Cassandra and James Austen's wife, Mary Lloyd, she had periods when her health rallied briefly, and it was during one of these, only three days before she died on 18 July, that this poem was written (or possibly dictated – the handwriting may not be hers). In the *Biographical Notice* Henry Austen refers to its 'stanzas replete with fancy and vigour', and the deft interweaving of the association of St Swithun and forty days' rain with Winchester races reveals a mind unimpaired by bodily illness. The shift in tone from the mock-social ('the weather was charming') to the comically melodramatic leads to a resolution of the old Saint's curse in nothing more terrible than 'July in showers'. Is it possible that something else was being resolved here? Those who, 'by vice...enslaved', have 'sinn'd...must suffer'; yet the 'curse' they will meet 'in [their] pleasures' is only rain – 'the gentle rain from heaven', perhaps? At the end of the second MS, possibly earlier (see textual note), someone

85

has added 'written July 15th 1817: by Jane Austen who died early in the morning (½ past 4) of July 18th 1817 aged 41 y^{rs}; and in this version the words 'When once we are buried you think we are gone [sic]/But behold me immortal!' have been – surely significantly – underlined.

1 *Winchester races* Steeplechases were held under civic patronage at Worthy Down, 3 miles north of the city, from the seventeenth century; Charles II preferred the racecourse even to Newmarket. JA could have seen the advertisement in the *Hampshire Chronicle* of Monday 14 July for the meeting to be held at the end of the month: 'His Majesty's Plate of 100 guineas on Tuesday 29 July, the City Plate of 50 guineas on 30 July, and the Cup of 90 guineas on 31 July'. Racing at Winchester ceased before the end of the nineteenth century, though a course still exists on Worthy Down and is used for exercising and training.

2 *their old Saint* Swithun (or Swithin), Bishop of Winchester, died in 862 and was buried in a simple grave outside the West Door of the Old Minster (see p.100). On 15 July 971 his remains were removed to a new shrine inside the cathedral, and a tradition grew up that a sudden storm during the ceremony showed that the humble Swithun was angry at the 'translation', hence the legend that St Swithun's Day determines the weather for the forty days following:

> St Swithin's day, gif ye do rain, for forty days it
> will remain;
> St Swithin's day an ye be fair, for forty days 'twill
> rain nae mair.

4 *William of Wykham* Bishop of Winchester 1367-1404 (see p.100).

10 *his shrine* In the Middle Ages, the remains of St Swithun were displayed on a platform behind the high altar, and subsequently in a new shrine in the retrochoir, until its destruction in 1538.

11 *the Palace* The ruins of the twelfth-century bishops' palace of Wolvesey lie about 300 yards to the south-east of the cathedral. The old Saint made a considerable spring.

13 *Venta* Venta Belgarum was the Roman name for Winchester.

18 *a neighbouring Plain* Worthy Down (see note above).

18 RIDDLES. [Solutions: 1. Hemlock. 2. Agent. 3. Banknote.]

19 CHARADE. [Solution: Courtship.] Emma comments: ' "I have read worse charades" '.

20 LINES *SUPPOSED* TO HAVE BEEN SENT TO AN UNCIVIL DRESSMAKER. Martha Lloyd, sister of James Austen's second wife, Mary, lived with her widowed mother at Ibthorpe, near Hurstbourne Tarrant, Hants. When Mrs Lloyd died, on 16 April 1805, Cassandra had been helping Martha and the Lloyds' companion, Mrs Stent, to nurse her for several weeks; in a letter of 21 April JA thanked her sister for writing on the previous day, which was 'quite an unexpected pleasure'. Martha's difficulties in having her mourning made up in time may well have been discussed either in that or in an earlier letter from Cassandra. Whether or not these verses by JA and Mrs Austen were sent to Ibthorpe is not known.

1   *sent to Miss Green*   Gowns and pelisses were often made up by professional dressmakers from material sent by the customer; on the death of her sister-in-law, Elizabeth Austen (see p.90), JA wrote: 'My mourning... will not impoverish me, for by having my velvet Pelisse fresh lined & made up, I am sure I shall have no occasion *this winter* for anything new of that sort. — I take my Cloak for the Lining... *One* Miss Baker makes my gown, & the other my Bonnet, which is to be silk covered with Crepe' (*Letters*, p.148).

3   *Black Ploughman's Gauze*   Possibly the 'special variant of black crape for mourning [that] was prepared from gummed yarn and had an embossed "figure" which produced a duller, denser texture' (Penelope Byrde, *A Frivolous Distinction*, Bath, 1979). In the letter cited above, JA writes: '*I* am to be in Bombazeen & Crape, according to what is universal *here*'; and in a letter of July 1811, Mrs Austen writes to Mary Lloyd: 'You are very bold to buy *Colour'd shoes*, last week I bought a Bombazeen, thinking I should get it cheaper than when the poor King was actually dead. If I outlive him it will answer my purpose. If I do not, somebody may mourn for me in it — it will be wanted for one or the other, I dare say, before the moths have eaten it up' (Hampshire Record Office, 23M93/62/2).

8   *This license to mourn & to grieve*   JA's lightness here perhaps suggests that the verses were not sent to Martha; but Mrs Lloyd was 76 and 'from repeated paralytic seizures had been failing in mind and body for some time past' (*Reminiscences*, p.7). The letter to Ibthorpe suggests that Cassandra felt Martha had accepted her loss: 'Your account of Martha is very comfortable indeed, & now we shall be in no fear of receiving a worse. This day, if she has gone to Church, must have been a trial of her feelings, but I hope it will be the last of

any acuteness.' And remarks about Mrs Lloyd's companion reveal her habitual irony: 'Poor M[rs] Stent! it has been her lot to be always in the way; but we must be merciful, for perhaps in time we may come to be M[rs] Stents ourselves, unequal to anything & unwelcome to everybody' (*Letters*, p.103). In any case, in a letter written a few days before Mrs Lloyd's death, JA makes her attitude clear: 'The Nonsense I have been writing in this & my last letter, seems out of place at such a time; but I will not mind it, it will do you no harm, & nobody else will be attacked by it' (*Letters*, p.100).

20 MISS GREEN'S REPLY.

14 *Or my name is not Green!* Mrs Austen neatly ends her verse with a return to the opening of JA's.

21 VERSES TO RHYME WITH 'ROSE'. This set of verses was probably written during the visit that Mrs Austen and her daughters paid in late August-September 1807 to Edward and his family, who were staying in Chawton Great House. For the problem of dating the MS see textual note.

21 [Mrs Austen] Mrs Austen contributes to the game an engagingly insouciant account of her daily labours.

6 *hose* Stockings of silk or cotton. Penelope Ruddock, of the Bath Museum of Costume, suggests that the shorter woollen, or possibly cotton, sock, of which Mrs Austen would 'rather have knit twenty Rows', could have been intended for a man or a boy; one of Edward's children seems the likeliest recipient.

10 *the Bucks & the Does* The well-stocked park and the reference to a library may be merely invention, but if they are to be taken as literal, it is evidence for the verses having been written during the visit to Chawton Great House.

17 *stupid* tiresome, dull. The wit of the final line shows this to be far from true!

22 [Miss Austen] Cassandra's attempt seems rather unsure of itself; not only is the comic effect of the red nose unfortunate, but it is difficult to see how even the most blustery wind could really change 'those/Who once were friends to bitter foes' (is there an echo of Amiens in *As You Like It*? – he tells us that the winter wind is *not* 'so unkind/As man's ingratitude').

22 [Miss J. Austen] JA sketches a living character who, even in his anonymity, strikes us as being completely true: the Sunday clothes; the prodigious rose in his buttonhole and the admiring glances he repeatedly gives it; the cheerfully un-pious churchgoing. It would never occur to him to envy 'the gayest London beaux', yet the comical implication is that he cares for his appearance just as much as they do for theirs. Though he comes to the service with both reverence and pleasure, he understands little of it; soothed rather than edified by the sermon, he 'rouses joyous' not at its divine exhortation but at its 'welcome close'. JA's amused and tolerant sympathy for this truly happy man is richly human.

2   *light-drab*   made of light brown cloth. Brown coats were much in fashion in the period.

2   *well-darn'd Hose*   JA is stressing here not his poverty, since in a thrifty age stockings would always have been repaired (see Mrs Austen's verse, above), but the fact that he keeps his clothes in good order.

5   *Cabbage rose*   'A double red rose, with a large round compact flower (*Rosa centifolia*)' (OED).

7   *London Beaux*   In *S&S* Miss Steele has to make do with provincial ones such as 'Mr. Rose at Exeter, a prodigious smart young man, quite a beau ... and yet if you do but meet him of a morning, he is not fit to be seen'. She thinks beaux 'vastly agreeable, provided they dress smart and behave civil', but she 'can't bear to see them dirty and nasty'. The sensible Elinor Dashwood, asked by Miss Steele if her brother wasn't quite a beau 'as he was so rich', replies, 'I cannot tell you, for I do not perfectly comprehend the meaning of the word' (*S&S* vol.I, ch.21, pp.123-4).

8   *among the rows*   In the ordinary pews, rather than in one of the high box-pews reserved for the well-to-do families – a distinction that existed in Chawton church at that date: 'In 1733 alterations were made in the Church internally. There is a memorandum signed by Jo. Baker, the Rector, to the following effect:– "This Church was New Pewed and Repaired by Bulstrode Knight Esq., and Elizabeth his wife, and the Parishioners seated by order of a Vestry, which Vestry is signed by the Minister and Churchwardens." The arrangement of seats begins as follows:– "*On the North side* Mr. Knight's Seat. *On the South Side* Mrs. Fisher's Seat. (⅔ the size of Mr. Knight's)." These were high square pews, which were converted into three and two pews respectively about 1859. Eight more pews were allotted on the north side and nine more on the south side; the men as a rule sitting on the north side and the women on the south' (W. Austen Leigh and Montagu G. Knight, *Chawton Manor and its Owners*, London, 1911, pp. 56-7).

23 [Mrs E. Austen] On 9 October 1808, eleven days after the birth of her last child, Brook John, Elizabeth Austen died suddenly. JA wrote, 'We need not enter into a Panegyric on the Departed — but it is sweet to think of her great worth — of her solid principles, her true devotion, her excellence in every relation of Life' (*Letters*, p.147). Since the verse to Miss Bigg with the pocket handkerchiefs which precedes this in the Bodmer MS is headed 'previous to her marriage' (see p.65) and that marriage took place on 25 October 1808, JA must have copied these verses after her sister-in-law's death, no doubt wishing to preserve the results of a happy family game from the summer of the previous year.

6 *feign* A misspelling of 'fain'.

6 *dispose* If 'hand over' is meant, an object is needed; if the sense is 'comply', the meaning is being stretched somewhat, since the OED records no such usage.

7 *the Muse who bestows/The gift of Poetry* Calliope. She was perhaps a little unresponsive on the present occasion.

23 BOUTS-RIMÉS. The preface to *Bouts-Rimés and Noun Verses* (by R.A. Austen-Leigh) records how the game was played: 'When the words for the Bouts-rimés had been settled by one or more members of the party, a certain time, perhaps half-an-hour, was allowed for writing them. All, when finished, were signed, folded up and handed in to the person chosen to be the reader. He looked them through himself, and when all had been sent in, he read them aloud to the company. On the first reading no guessing as to the Authors was allowed. He then read them aloud again, pausing at the end of each, till the Author had been guessed. Contributors might send in as many as they pleased.'

[Mrs Austen 2]

1 *I've said it in prose* An empty purse is a favourite theme with the prudent Mrs Austen (see 'I hope, my Anna', p.34); in 1820 her financial circumstances had not been particularly comfortable for some years, and the omission of any legacy in the will of her wealthy brother, James Leigh Perrot, who died childless in 1817, had been a great disappointment.

[George Knight 2]

3 *Talma* François-Joseph Talma (1763-1826), French tragic actor.

25 EPISTLE TO G. EAST ESQ^R   The kindly and conscientious concern that Mrs Austen showed for her husband's pupils in the household is evident here; while not underrating for a moment the value of learning, she can sympathise with the feelings of a young man of fifteen who prefers dancing to books. By jokingly including herself among the enthusiastic students of the mansion of learning, and by reducing Virgilian epic to a story that is 'quite entertaining', she acknowledges at once the importance and the uncongeniality of study.

11   *and creates fresh delays*   She knows her man.

28   *Romance*   A novel.

31   *'Cassandra'*   *Cassandra, Heroine of Romance*, a novel set in the time of Alexander the Great, by G. de Costes de la Calprenède; the popular English translation was by Sir Charles Cotterell (1653).

54   *Fowle, Stewart, Deane*   The other three pupils currently resident in the rectory: Fulwar Craven Fowle, eldest son of the Revd Thomas Fowle, vicar of Kintbury, Berks; Frank Stuart ('presumably the son of the Mr James Stuart whom Mr Austen had chosen as godfather for Charles' [*Fam. Rec.*, p.39]); and either George or Henry Deane, whose father was Mr Henry Deane of Reading. Whether or not the errant Gilbert East did return, his father presented Mr Austen with a picture; in January 1801, when the family were preparing to move to Bath, JA wrote: 'As to our Pictures, the Battlepiece, Mr Nibbs, Sir Wm East, & all the old heterogenous miscellany, manuscript, Scriptoral peices dispersed over the House are to be given to James' (*Letters*, p.67).

54   *Henry & Ned*   James Austen had gone up to Oxford earlier that year; George, who was mentally handicapped, never lived at home; and Francis was only five years old. Since this is an 'epistle', Mrs Austen deftly uses the five names to sign off.

27 TO F.S.   Anna Lefroy's description of her grandmother's verse as 'making no pretence to poetry, but being simply playful common sense in rhyme' is certainly borne out by this teasing, yet wise, rebuke to one of her husband's pupils, who exhibited jealousy of one of the others. The Fowle family were close to the Austens, however, the Revd Thomas Fowle having been at university with Mr Austen: all his four sons became pupils at the rectory; Fulwar Craven was a close friend of James, who dedicated a grandiose poem to him; and the second son, Thomas, became engaged to Cassandra in 1792. The accusation of 'partiality' against Mrs Austen may therefore have been justified; certainly the fourth verse seems to suggest as much.

    F.S.   Frank Stuart (see p.91).

24 *'Serve that man first who first is'*   Cf. proverb: 'First born, first fed'.

28 THE HUMBLE PETITION OF R^D BULLER & W. GOODENOUGH   In incorporating into their 'petition' the promise 'to study hard every day', Mrs Austen may have gone further than the boys intended!

    R^d Buller   Richard Buller, son of the Bishop of Exeter, was a pupil of Mr Austen 1790-5.

    W. Goodenough   From Winterbourne Stoke, Wiltshire (*Fam. Rec.*, p.68).

3 *creaking old weathercock*   Describing Steventon Rectory, Anna Lefroy wrote: 'near the Wood Walk gate, and garden bench adjoining, was placed a tall white pole surmounted by a weather-cock. How pleasant to childish ears was the scrooping sound of that weathercock, moved by the summer breeze!' (Lefroy MS, quoted in *Fam. Rec.*, p.18.)

29 I SEND YOU HERE.   When she was away from home, JA liked to hear news of the assemblies; in a letter to Cassandra at Godmersham of 30 November 1800, for example, when she was staying with the Lloyds at Ibthorpe, she wrote: 'I have charged my Myrmidons to send me an account of the Basingstoke Ball [of 27 November]; I have placed my spies at different places that they may collect the more; & by so doing, by sending Miss Bigg to the Townhall itself, & posting my Mother at Steventon I hope to derive from their various observations a good general idea of the whole' (*Letters*, p.65). In this verse Mrs Austen not only juggles the names adroitly but also adds some genially crisp comments on the list: the witty ingenuity of the rhyme 'Sister/. . . who'd have missed her?' tempers the offhand asperity of the sentiment; and her censure of Squire Le Fevre for causing the Dorchesters to miss the ball is chattily transferred to the General, who 'would not stay', thereby upsetting the arrangements. Incidentally, 'it is not clever' must have been a favourite phrase of Mrs Austen's (see the 'Epistle to G. East', p.26); here, as so often, we catch her tone of voice.

    1794   The two surviving MSS are in the hand of Anna Lefroy (see textual note), who in transcribing the poem seems to have made a mistake with the year, since Lord Dorchester was in Quebec from Sept. 1793 to July 1796; furthermore on the date suggested in *Fam. Rec.* (p.79), 16 Jan. 1794, not only did Cassandra and Henry attend the ball, but Eliza Chute's diary records the presence of three persons not mentioned in the poem. The correct reading may be 1796 – four balls were held on Thursdays in that year; or the lines may possibly be about some occasion after 1800, when the balls began to be advertised as 'Subscription Assemblies' (see Robin Vick, 'The Basingstoke Assemblies', Jane Austen Society *Report* for 1993) – Mrs Austen makes it clear that both Lord Dorchester and Squire LeFevre were subscribers.

6   *the couple from the Vine*   William John Chute MP and his wife Elizabeth (née Smith) of The Vyne, Sherborne St John, near Basingstoke.

7   *Squire Hicks*   Michael Hicks was married to Henrietta-Maria Beach ('his fair spouse'), first cousin of Wither Bramston, below.

8   *M.r Bramston's house*   Oakley Hall, near Basingstoke. Wither Bramston had married Mary Chute of The Vyne, but they had no children and Oakley Hall passed in 1832 to William Hicks-Beach.

9   *Madam and her maiden Sister*   Mrs Bramston and an unmarried Chute sister.

11   *Miss Woodward*   Possibly a companion to the childless Mrs Bramston, who at that time was a woman of thirty.

13   *Alethea*   Alethea Bigg, sister to Catherine, to whom JA sent the handkerchiefs (see p.7). The Bigg-Withers, of Manydown Park, were related to the Hicks-Beaches.

13   *Harriet*   Possibly Harriet Heathcote, of Hursley Park, whose brother William married Elizabeth Bigg in 1798. JA saw her, apparently for the first time, at a ball at Deane House in January 1796, when she described her as 'pretty, but not near so handsome as I expected' (*Letters*, p.1).

14   *chariot*   'Applied in 18th c. to a light four-wheeled carriage with only back seats, and differing from the post-chaise in having a coach-box.' (OED)

15   *Perhaps they did*   Mrs Austen may be reflecting that seven passengers in the carriage might have been rather a squeeze.

16   *4 good folk from Worting*   Mr and Mrs John Clarke of Worting, near Basingstoke, were old friends of Mr and Mrs George Hoar, who also lived there. JA met the Hoars when calling on the Clarkes in December 1798 (*Letters*, p.29).

19   *Lefroy*   JA's great friend, Anne Lefroy (see *To the Memory of M.rs Lefroy*), was the wife of the Revd Isaac Lefroy, rector of Ashe. The eldest of their seven children, Jemima Lucy, would have been fourteen in 1794 (but see note on the date, above).

20 *Henry Rice, that pleasant boy*   Lucy must also have found him plea-
sant, for she married him in 1801. He was sued for debt by his
brother-in-law in 1812, and in 1819 fled to Dunkirk.

22 *Sir Colebrook*   Sir George Colebrooke, Bt.

22 *Sir Grant*   Sir Alexander Grant of Dalvey, Bt., of Malshanger House
near Worting; the Grants were related by marriage with the Cole-
brookes.

23 *Miss Eyre of Sherfield*   Neither Miss Eyre nor her Mother can be
identified. Sherfield on Loddon is a village to the NE of Basingstoke.

24 *One Miss from Dummer*   In the Terry family, of Dummer, near
Basingstoke, there were thirteen children, of whom the eldest,
Stephen, wrote *The Diaries of Dummer* (see p.69) and the second, the
Revd Michael, was at one time engaged to Anna Lefroy (see p.83).

26 *Mʳ & Mʳˢ Williamson*   Unidentified.

27 *Charles Powlett*   Rector of Winslade, Hampshire. A grandson of the
3rd Duke of Bolton, he eventually became Chaplain-in-Ordinary
to the Prince of Wales. He was a man of extravagant tastes; JA
writes to Cassandra, 19 December 1798, 'Charles Powlett gave a
dance on Thursday, to the great disturbance of all his neighbours,
of course, who, you know, take a most lively interest in the state of
his finances, and live in hopes of his being soon ruined' (*Letters*,
p.25).

27 *his pupils twain*   It is possible that the Revd William Hasker, curate
of Baughurst, and Mr Edward Lane of Worting, a connection of the
Bigg-Withers, had been pupils of Charles Powlett; on the other
hand, Mrs Austen's 'six & thirty folk' suggests that the 'pupils
twain' were in addition.

29 *Bentworth's Rector*   Revd John Calland, rector of Bentworth, near
Alton. After a ball in December 1798 JA wrote: 'Mʳ Calland...
appeared as usual with his hat in his hand, & stood every now &
then behind Catherine [Bigg] & me to be talked to & abused for not
dancing. — We teized him however into it at last; — I was very glad
to see him again after so long a separation, & he was altogether
rather the Genius & Flirt of the Evening' (*Letters*, p.29).

31 *Misses Davies*   Unidentified. A connection with the Mrs Davies
who 'frightened' Charles Austen 'into buying a piece of Irish [linen]'
when he and JA were in Basingstoke (*Letters*, p.38) seems unlikely.

35 *The Dorchesters*   Guy Carleton, first Baron Dorchester, of Kempshott
Park, Basingstoke, married 1772 Maria, daughter of 2nd Earl of Effing-
ham. C.-in-C. in America 1781-3, Governor of Quebec until 1796.

37 *Squire LeFevre* Charles Shaw-Lefevre MP, of Heckfield Place, Hampshire.

41 *General Donne* Emma Austen-Leigh (*Jane Austen and Steventon*) suggests Sir George Don (1754-1832), but it is more likely that Mrs Austen misheard and that 'his Lordship's old companion' was Lt-General Sir David Dundas, who, like Lord Dorchester, had been at the Siege of Havana in 1762.

30 DIALOGUE BETWEEN DEATH AND M^{RS} A.   This verse is followed in the MS by three fables adapted from Æsop (see below); and, in the personification of Death, the 'Dialogue' is also in the form of a fable. The movement from a teasing familiarity with the character of Death (as in Fable 3) to the tribute to the love and care shown by Mrs Austen's family is effected through an expanding stanza, where the additional line slows down the pace in order to modulate to a more serious mood; the last line only partially disturbs this, with its audacious rhyme half comically putting up the good doctor who saved her as an abler practitioner than the unsuccessful Death.

3 *turn'd of threescore* Mrs Austen was sixty-four.
9 *BOWEN* William Bowen, of Spry & Bowen, apothecaries, 1 Argyle Buildings, Bath, who was also in attendance on Mr Austen in his final illness a year later: 'Dr Gibbs & Mr Bowen had scarcely left his room before he sunk into a Sleep from which he never woke' (JA, letter to Francis Austen, 22 January 1805, *Letters*, p.97).

31 FABLES.   Gay's *Fables* were published in two sets, in respectively 1727 and 1738, and immediately became immensely popular. If the Austens did not possess a copy (which is unlikely), they would have known them from the ones reprinted in *Elegant Extracts*; but Mrs Austen, like Catherine Morland, who 'learnt the fable of "The Hare and many Friends," as quickly as any girl in England' (*NA*, ch.1, p.14), was probably brought up with them. Her three attempts have the same metre as Gay's, yet as so often one catches her very personal tone of voice – in the chatty aside telling us that the stone was 'worth at least a hundred pound', or in the sense of incredulity at the Country man's great age, the use of the present tense making him seem to be a real person whom she has heard about.

32 A RECEIPT FOR A PUDDING.   The allusion to 'the vicar' indicates that the verse Martha Lloyd copied into her recipe book may have dated from before Mr Austen's death in January 1805; on the other hand, the act of turning a simple domestic recipe into a poem may have required a brief introduction of this kind. The final joke is characteristic of Mrs Austen's instinct for the ending of a verse (see the 'Epistle to G. East').

    A receipt for a Pudding   Hannah Glasse gives a comparable recipe: 'Cut off all the crust of a penny white-loaf, and slice it thin into a quart of milk, set it over a chafing-dish of coals till the bread has soaked up all the milk, then put in a piece of sweet butter, stir it round, let it stand till cool; or you may boil your milk, and pour over your bread and cover it up close, does full as well; then take the yolks of six eggs, the whites of three, and beat them up with a little rose-water and nutmeg, a little salt and sugar, if you choose it. Mix all well together, and boil it one hour' (*The Art of Cookery, made Plain and Easy*, 1788 edn).

14   *currants... And sugar of each half a pound*   'The vicar' clearly had a very sweet tooth.

27   *A proper hint this for its maker*   See recipe above. The conversational tone is characteristic of Mrs Austen.

30   *With care recommend to the baker*   The kitchens at Steventon and Chawton had bread ovens, though some of the lodgings the Austens took in Bath may not have done; but it was quite usual for dishes to be sent out to the local baker, as Miss Bates does with the apples Mr Knightley sends her (*Emma*, vol.2, ch.9, p.238).

31   *this pudding*   The subsequent rhyme suggests the pronunciation 'pudd'n'.

33   *should you suspect a fond word*   In case you think I am expressing unreasoning praise.

36   *smoke*   I.e. steam.

39   *The other comes in out of season*   'If only one pudding is needed, the second one (which you made because you doubted this recipe) will be inopportune.'

34 I HOPE, MY ANNA.   Perhaps the most serious verse that has survived by Mrs Austen, these lines extend the particular wish for happiness in marriage to the invoking of eternal pardon and blessedness; only the practical acknowledgement of the impossibility of making her granddaughter richer reflects her habitual tone. The letter following the verse begins: 'My dear Anna, The above lines were composed last May, one Sunday evening when I was on the Sopha with the head-ache and you and your aunts [Jane and Cassandra] were sitting round the Table; you had just told me you should depend on my writing you a congratulatory Letter on your Marriage; what I then said in verse I now repeat in plain prose — may you both be very, very happy in this world, and perfectly so in the next.'

6 *My Grandson* The readiness with which Mrs Austen makes Anna's husband one of the family is significant. (For the circumstances of her engagement see p.82).

8 *I wish you an increase of wealth* A year earlier the question of Ben Lefroy's future had been causing great anxiety to James Austen; in October 1813 JA wrote to Cassandra: 'I have had a late account from Steventon, & a baddish one, as far as Ben is concerned. — He has declined a Curacy (apparently highly eligible) which he might have secured against his taking orders — & upon it's being made rather a serious question, says he has not made up his mind as to taking orders so early — & that if her Father makes a point of it, he must give Anna up rather than do what he does not approve. — He must be maddish' (*Letters*, p.246). He did take Holy Orders in 1817, eventually becoming rector of Ashe in 1823.

36 RIDDLES AND CHARADES.
1. [Solution: the letter W.]
9 *a chosen few* I.e. the letters of the word 'Wales'.
11 *rather crooked* The 's'.
12 *a Grenadier* The 'I' (the Grenadiers being known for their height).
Riddle 2ᵈ [Solution: kettle.]
12 *smart & neater* The small tea-kettle was brought into the drawing-room, where tea was kept locked in a caddy.
22 *scandal's friend* Cf. Congreve, *The Double Dealer*, Act 1 sc.1: '*Mellefont*. Why, [the women] are at the end of the gallery, retired to their tea and scandal, according to their ancient custom, after dinner.'
Riddle 3ᵈ. [Solution: the letter D.] The identity of the 'speaker' as a country gentleman fallen on hard times is carefully and consistently built up.
4 *the Ladies Diary* One of the many pocket-books published annually which, as well as being a diary, also included printed information. Ones belonging to both Mary Lloyd and Fanny Knight survive.
28 *is all you've said a Joke?* 'D' is now so well established as a person that he can be addressed; and in a particularly deft final line he is simultaneously gentleman and puzzle.
Riddle [4]. [Solution: the letter O.]
Riddle [5]. [Solution ox, beef, mork(e)in.]
I am grateful to Deirdre Le Faye for the solution to this ingenious riddle. The OED defines 'morkin' as 'a beast that dies by disease or accident' and gives several possible seven-letter spellings (necessary for the 'three letters more' added to the four of 'beef'), among them 'morkein' and

'mortkin'; 'morekin', though not listed, is attractive because it implies an added play on 'Three Letters *more*'. Alternatively, Mrs Austen may simply have intended to write 'Two Letters more'.

[6]. [Solution: Jack.]

1 *sometimes covered with soot* I.e. a mechanism for turning a spit activated by hot air in the chimney.

2 *of very great use at a feast* I.e. a serving-man.

4 *a Fish* The jack-fish, or pike.

4 *a beast* Jackass.

[7]. [Solution: Turnpike.]

[8]. [Solution: Merrythought.]

[9]. [Solution: Buckram.]

8 *'t'was once worn by a Prince* Prince Hal (see *1 Henry IV* Act 1, sc.2).

James Austen

40 EPILOGUE TO THE SULTAN. The tactics that in the play Roxalana practises so persuasively on the Sultan are here given a domestic setting. Although the dialogue does not take place at bedtime, it resembles a curtain lecture, as the phrase 'behind the connubial curtain' perhaps suggests. In fact it in many ways anticipates Douglas Jerrold's *Mrs. Caudle's Curtain Lectures*, which appeared in *Punch* in 1845 (Jerrold was a midshipman in Charles Austen's ship the *Namur* anchored at the Nore in 1813, and 'recalled that he owed his start to Captain Austen, "a relative of the novelist", when he became well known as a humorist' [*Honan*, p.332]; since there were both a library and a theatre on board, it is quite possible that he knew of James Austen's theatrical prologues and epilogues).

Miss Cooper Jane Cooper, daughter of Mrs Austen's sister Jane Leigh.

22 *the club* A periodic meeting of, in Johnson's phrase, 'good fellows' at a tavern. Mrs Caudle's opinions of her husband's joining such a club, 'the Skylarks', are the subject of the third *Curtain Lecture*.

33 *her husband who teazes* 'Who persistently vexes her husband.'

51 *Divan* The Turkish council of state presided over by the sultan; hence, here, the audience.

42 TO EDWARD ON THE DEATH OF HIS FIRST PONY. In what is perhaps the most touching of all his verses, James Austen shows his 'weeping boy' that the loss of the pony offers an opportunity to prepare his mind for the 'more serious ills of life'. Yet 'reason' teaches that only those ills 'which on ourselves we bring' can truly make us suffer, and 'every sorrow will be light,/ When all within our breasts is right'. This is precisely the sentiment that Colonel Brandon expresses about Marianne's betrayal by Willoughby: 'She will feel her own sufferings to be nothing. They proceed from no misconduct, and can bring no disgrace' (*S&S* vol.2, ch.9, p.210). *S&S* was published later the same year.

  2   *Pony dead*   '"Edward's pony died suddenly". I saw its dying struggles in the stable, having been taken out there by one of the maids, who hurried me off again directly. This was a great grief to my brother, and some to me. Pony was sorrowfully interred in a corner of the Home Meadow, and his grave was discernible for some years afterwards' (*Reminiscences*, p.25).

 12   *sain foin*   A low-growing forage plant.

 17   *sieve*   Basket or other kind of container here no doubt holding fodder.

 34   *corse*   Corpse.

 38   *His Father's hand in silence took*   This touchingly observed action is used as a fulcrum between the two long passages of speech.

45 TYGER'S LETTER TO CAROLINE.   With unmistakable sureness of touch James Austen locates the poem within the boundaries of the child's world – kitchen, bedroom, farm – and peoples it with the figures with whom she would be on terms of easy familiarity.

  5   *Harriet*   The cook.

 10   *I slept a little on the dough*   Thereby stopping it rising.

 39   *fat*   I.e. her healthy plumpness.

46 ADDRESS TO TYGER.

 10   *Micaenas*   A patron of the arts (from the adviser to Augustus and patron of Horace and Virgil).

 13   *when you slept upon the dough*   See 'Tyger's Letter to Caroline', above.

 32   *guttling appetite*   To guttle is 'to eat voraciously; to gormandize' (OED).

 43   *Corbet*   Farm bailiff at Steventon.

48 VENTA! WITHIN THY SACRED FANE.   As a young man James Austen had explored a vein of generalised melancholy in his 'Elegy Written at Kintbury Berks', a poem clearly influenced by Gray's famous 'Elegy Written in a Country Churchyard'. In this memorial to his sister the expression of feeling, though particularised, is held firmly in check, the 'bitter tear' dropped on her bier by her brothers conveying, as an image, a distinct impression of funereal marble. The poem reveals a clearly defined structure in which the opening address to the resting-place of the mighty provides a grandiose setting, architecturally and, in terms of the elegy, verbally, for the 'fair form and fairer mind' of the sister who is interred in both cathedral and poem; then, after a tribute to the literary and domestic labours that, creditably, she found not to be incompatible, the final section of the poem speculates on the nature of the human state after death, as, in the convention of elegy, her spirit is sent on its heaven-ward journey.

1   *Venta*   The Roman name for the city of Winchester.
    fane   Temple.

2   *many a chief*   The remains of Saxon kings originally buried in the Old Minster, which stood adjacent to the present cathedral, were transferred to mortuary chests placed over the presbytery screens in 1525.

6   *Gothic choir*   The construction of the great retrochoir at the beginning of the thirteenth century more than doubled the area of the original east end.
    pillared Aisle   I.e. the nave, with its soaring Perpendicular pillars.

10 *coffins*   The mortuary chests referred to above.

12 *the Conqueror's haughty Son*   A twelfth-century tomb in the choir is supposedly that of William Rufus.

15 *honoured Wickham*   William of Wykeham (*c.*1323-1404), Chancellor of England and founder of New College, Oxford and Winchester College, as Bishop of Winchester remodelled the original Norman nave of the cathedral.

18 *Old Walkelyn's heavier style*   The Norman bishop Walkelin was responsible for the Romanesque building.

38 *'Which dying, she would wish to blot'*   Cf. Ben Jonson's remark (in *Discoveries, De Shakespeare Nostrati*) of Shakespeare: 'in his writing (whatsoever he penned) he never blotted out a line'.

71 *By Seraphs born . . . While Angles gladden at the sight*   A conventional enough image (if a somewhat unconventional spelling, particularly for a clergyman), it gains a special appropriateness here by the presence at the other end of the North Aisle of the 'Guardian Angels' Chapel' with its thirteenth-century vault paintings of angels.

50 TO MISS JANE AUSTEN THE REPUTED AUTHOR OF SENSE AND SENSIBILITY.

1   *On such Subjects* I.e. sense and sensibility.

3   *Sterne's darling Maid* '— Dear sensibility! source inexhausted of all that's precious in our joys, or costly in our sorrows!' – Sterne, *A Sentimental Journey*, vol.2, 'The Bourbonnois'.

5   *Fair Elinor's Self* In *S&S* Elinor Dashwood embodies the quality of sense and her sister Marianne that of undisciplined feeling.

51 CHARADE. [Solution: Canterbury.]

3   *Curate* I.e. a clergyman (cf. *Book of Common Prayer*: 'Send down upon our Bishops and Curates, and all Congregations committed to their charge, the healthful Spirit of thy grace...').

James Leigh Perrot

52 ON CAPT. FOOTE'S MARRIAGE WITH MISS PATTON.   The fortuitous coincidence of names leads to a happy explosion of puns arising from the different parts of the patten.

  Capt. Foote Edward James Foote, Captain RN (later Vice-Admiral), married as his second wife Mary, daughter of Admiral Patton. Captain Foote was a friend of Francis Austen, and JA recorded in 'Opinions of *Mansfield Park*' that he was 'surprised that I had the power of drawing the Portsmouth Scenes so well' (*MW* p.435).

1   *patten* A piece of wood mounted on an iron ring and attached to the foot by a leather loop (here *knot*) to *guard* the shoe against mud and wet.

4   *Clog* Wooden soled overshoe (without the ring); a block of wood fastened to the leg to impede movement.

52 RIDDLES.   1. [Solution: Pair of spurs.]
2. [Solution: Repeating watch.] This riddle makes a bravura display of puns (cf. the lines on the marriage of Capt. Foote).
3. [Solution: Knife.]

Cassandra Elizabeth Austen

54 CHARADES.   [Solutions: 1. Liquorice. 2. Baronet.]

Francis William Austen

54 CHARADE.   [Solution: Season.]

Charles John Austen

55 CHARADE.   [Solution: A light.]

Henry Thomas Austen

55 CHARADE.   [Solution: Patriot.]
  6 *great Chatham's name*   William Pitt, the Elder, 1st Earl of Chatham,
     who led the Patriot faction of the Whigs. (For an amusing Victorian
     bowdlerisation of this charade, see textual note.)

56 GODMERSHAM THE TEMPLE OF DELIGHT.
  2 *Open is the gate to thee*   The pier gate through which JA described
     Francis and Mary Austen driving after their marriage (see p.5).

George Knight

56 GEORGE KNIGHT TO HIS DOG PINCHER.
     Pincher   A popular name to call a hunting dog, from its assiduous-
     ness in 'pinching' or harrying the quarry.

Jane Anna Elizabeth Austen (Anna Lefroy)

57 ON READING A LETTER.   For the background to this and the next poem
see p.82 and for a more detailed account, see Margaret Wilson, 'Anna
Austen's poems and her attachment to Mr Terry' in JA Society *Report* for
1987, pp.21-8.

Fanny Knight

57 TO ANNA ELIZA AUSTEN.   A strong religious upbringing and the early
loss of her mother (see p.90) produced in Fanny Austen a tendency to
introspection; in her diary at the end of 1809 she wrote, 'I am afraid I have
not improved much in any respect this last year; my faults are very great
and I have often indulged them shamefully' (quoted in Margaret Wilson,
Almost another sister, Maidstone, 1990, p.22). She clearly feels that her
cousin, brooding on Mr Terry, has every reason also to reflect on what
the past year has brought.

15 *This chequered scene of woes* Cf. 'This life is all chequer'd with pleasures and woes' in the 4th number of Moore's *Irish Melodies* (which however was not published until Nov. 1811).

James Edward Austen-Leigh

58 LINES ADDRESSED TO HIS FATHER ON MAKING HIM A PRESENT OF A KNIFE.
2 *if a Knife you give away* 'The commonest modern superstition about knives is that, because they are sharp-cutting, they sever love or friendship when given as a present. They should never be accepted without something being given in exchange.' (E. & M.A. Radford, ed. Hole, *Encyclopaedia of Superstitions*, London, 1961.)

59 DIRT & SLIME.
3 *Kintbury* The Revd Fulwar Craven Fowle, a close friend of James Austen from childhood (see p.91), was vicar of Kintbury, Berkshire.
4 *Some very pretty verses* '*Home* Written on returning from Kintbury — Sep.^t 1812'. The poem begins:

> Through Berkshire's lanes & hedgerows green,
> When, the spreading oaks between,
> Peeps the landscape's varied charm,
> Cornfield, mead, or sheltered farm,
> Intervening copse & heath
> In gay confusion, & beneath
> The shelter of each sloping hill,
> Many a little nameless rill
> Through alders dark, or willows gray,
> Or rushes, works its tangled way;
> Hasty through these fair scenes I passed...

Though James Austen describes the scenery through which he passes, the concern of the poem is with the attraction of home.
9 *Bays* In classical times poets were crowned with garlands of bay leaves.
37 *Thus when a good & steady hound* The young James Edward was a keen hunter. The following year, when he was being prepared for entry to Winchester, his father wrote a poem for him 'On refusing a special invitation from Mr Chute to meet his hounds':

> 'Why must this day be spent in books?'
> If I interpret right his looks,
>   My Edward seems to say;

'Why rest our horses in the stable,
To carry us completely able,
        O! why not hunt to day?'...

Let you and me meanwhile my Boy
In books at home our hours employ,
        And learn what we are able;
At Winton else you'll roughly fare,
When you are placed beneath the care
        Of Dr Henry Gabell.

54   *ran the heel*   Ran back on the scent.

61 TO MISS J. AUSTEN.

9   *Mrs Jennings... the Middletons, Dashwoods*   In *S&S*.

13   *cottages*   For Robert Ferrars's grandiose conception of a 'cottage' see *S&S* vol.II, ch.14, pp.251-2.

14   *Mr. Collins... Lady de Bourgh*   In *P&P*.

19   *Your works to Sir William pray send*   Sir William Welby was a cousin of Mrs Leigh Perrot and also father-in-law of her niece Wilhelmina, whom in 1801 JA reported as 'singing Duetts with the Prince of Wales' (*Letters* p.74). Mrs Leigh Perrot and her husband were fond of their nephew James, and her talk of Sir William and other grand acquaintances would no doubt have become something of a joke among the younger members of his family. JA may not have been amused by the reference as she disliked her aunt, and was furthermore disappointed that Mr Leigh Perrot, having come into a large augmentation of his already considerable fortune, should make an allowance to James, who as rector of Steventon was quite comfortably off, while her mother was passed over.

25   *becoming his wife*   The Princess of Wales had been the subject of much discussion since the publication in the newspapers earlier in the year of a letter from her to the Prince Regent protesting at his refusal to allow her visiting rights to their daughter, the Princess Charlotte; on 16 February 1813 JA had written to Martha Lloyd: 'I suppose all the World is sitting in Judgement on the Princess of Wales's Letter. Poor Woman, I shall support her as long as I can, because she *is* a Woman, & because I hate her Husband...' (*Letters* p.208). Two years later, JA was obliged to dedicate *Emma* to him.

62 NOUN VERSE.   'For Noun Verses two slips of papers had to be prepared for each player, a larger and a smaller slip; on the former he wrote a question and on the latter a noun. Both slips were folded up lengthways so as to hide the writing. They were then handed round, separately, and everyone drew a question and a noun, without seeing either beforehand, and had to write an answer to the question in verse, bringing in the noun. When finished they were read out' (R.A. Austen-Leigh, preface to *Bouts-Rimés and Noun Verses*).

2   *to see her thus display it*   I.e. Fanny Price.

4   *Mrs. Grant*   See *MP*.

APPENDIX

The following poems, not composed by Jane Austen, exist in copies in her hand:

ON THE UNIVERSITIES (anon. first publ. *Elegant Extracts*, 1789):
New York Public Library, Berg Collection.

ON CAPT. FOOTE'S MARRIAGE WITH MISS PATTON (James Leigh Perrot):
see p.75.

LINES OF LORD BYRON, IN THE CHARACTER OF BUONAPARTÉ (Byron):
Southampton University Library.

CHARADE BY A LADY (Catherine Maria Fanshawe):
Warden and Fellows' Library, Winchester College.

KALENDAR OF FLORA (source unidentified):
Descendants of Admiral Charles Austen.
The nine verses of this poem trace the appearance of various flowers through the cycle of the seasons, concluding with the pious sentiment that 'All are for Use, for Health or Pleasure given,/All speak in various ways the bounteous hand of Heaven'. The style is formal and stilted (many of the plants are referred to by their Latin names) and presumably Jane Austen's interest in it was botanical rather than literary.

THOMAS CHATTERTON (1752-1770)
Selected Poems
edited by Grevel Lindop

JOHN CLARE (1793-1864)
Northborough Sonnets
edited by Eric Robinson, David Powell and P.M.S. Dawson

The Midsummer Cushion
edited by R.K.R. Thornton and Anne Tibble

Northborough Sonnets
edited by Eric Robinson, David Powell and P.M.S. Dawson

ARTHUR HUGH CLOUGH (1819-1861)
Selected Poems
edited by Shirley Chew

SAMUEL TAYLOR COLERIDGE (1772-1834)
Selected Poetry
edited by William Empson and David Pirie

ABRAHAM COWLEY (1618-1667)
Selected Poems
edited by David Hopkins and Tom Mason

WILLIAM COWPER (1731-1800)
Selected Poems
edited by Nicholas Rhodes

GEORGE CRABBE (1754-1832)
Selected Poems
edited by Jem Poster

ANNE FINCH, COUNTESS OF WINCHILSEA
(1661-1720)
Selected Poems
edited by Denys Thompson

JOHN GAY (1685-1732)
Selected Poems
edited by Marcus Walsh

OLIVER GOLDSMITH (?1730-1774)
Selected Poems
edited by John Lucas

JOHN GOWER (1330-1408)
Selected Poetry
edited by Carole Weinberg

THOMAS GRAY (1716-1771)
Selected Poems
edited by John Heath-Stubbs

FULKE GREVILLE (1554-1628)
Selected Poems
edited by Neil Powell

IVOR GURNEY (1890-1937)
Best Poems *and*
The Book of Five Makings
edited by R.K.R. Thornton

ROBERT HENRYSON (?1425-1508?)
Selected Poems
edited by W.R.J. Barron

ROBERT HERRICK (1591-1674)
Selected Poems
edited by David Jesson-Dibley

NICHOLAS HILLIARD (1546/7-1618)
The Arte of Limning
edited by R.K.R. Thornton and T.G.S. Cain

THOMAS HOOD (1799-1845)
Selected Poems
edited by Joy Flint

RICHARD HOOKER (1553/4-1600)
Ecclesiastical Polity: selections
edited by Arthur Pollard

LEIGH HUNT (1784-1859)
Selected Writings
edited by David Jesson-Dibley

BEN JONSON (1572-1637)
Epigrams & The Forest
edited by Richard Dutton

CHARLES LAMB (1775-1834)
Charles Lamb and Elia
edited by J.E. Morpurgo

WILLIAM LAW (1686-1761)
Selected Writings
edited by Janet Louth

RICHARD LOVELACE (1618-1658)
Selected Poems
edited by Gerald Hammond

ANDREW MARVELL (1621-1678)
Selected Poems
edited by Bill Hutchings

JOHN MASEFIELD (1878-1967)
Selected Poems
edited by Donald Stanford

GEORGE MEREDITH (1828-1909)
Selected Poems
edited by Keith Hanley

WILLIAM MORRIS (1834-1896)
Selected Poems
edited by Peter Faulkner

EDGAR ALLAN POE (1809-1849)
Poems and Essays on Poetry
edited by C.H. Sisson

JOHN WILMOT, EARL OF ROCHESTER
(1648-1680)
The Debt to Pleasure
edited by John Adlard

CHRISTINA ROSSETTI (1830-1894)
Selected Poems
edited by C.H. Sisson

DANTE GABRIEL ROSSETTI (1828-1892)
Selected Poems and Translations
edited by Clive Wilmer

SIR WALTER SCOTT (1771-1832)
Selected Poems
edited by James Reed

MARY SIDNEY, COUNTESS OF PEMBROKE
(1561-1621) and SIR PHILIP SIDNEY
(1554-1586)
The Sidney Psalms
edited by R.E. Pritchard

SIR PHILIP SIDNEY (1554-1586)
Selected Writings
edited by Richard Dutton

JOHN SKELTON (1460-1529)
Selected Poems
edited by Gerald Hammond

CHRISTOPHER SMART (1722-1771)
The Religious Poetry
edited by Marcus Walsh

HENRY HOWARD, EARL OF SURREY
(1517-1547)
Selected Poems
edited by Dennis Keene

JONATHAN SWIFT (1667-1745)
Selected Poems
edited by C.H. Sisson

ALGERNON CHARLES SWINBURNE
(1837-1909)
Selected Poems
edited by L.M. Findlay

ARTHUR SYMONS (1865-1945)
Selected Writings
edited by R.V. Holdsworth

JEREMY TAYLOR (1613-1667)
Selected Writings
edited by C.H. Sisson

THOMAS TRAHERNE (?1637-1674)
Selected Writings
edited by Dick Davis

HENRY VAUGHAN (1622-1695)
Selected Poems
edited by Robert B. Shaw

JAMES McNEILL WHISTLER (1834-1903)
Whistler on Art
edited by Nigel Thorp

OSCAR WILDE (1854-1900)
Selected Poems
edited by Malcolm Hicks

'Carcanet are doing an excellent job in this series: the editions are labours of love, not just commercial enterprises. I hope they are familiar to all readers and teachers of literature.' – *Times Literary Supplement*